WHAT JESUS SAID
ABOUT MONEY AND POSSESSIONS

Keith Tondeur is director of Credit Action in Cambridge, author of several books including *Debt Free Living* (Monarch) and a popular speaker.

'Many people are impoverished because they haven't learned how to handle money. This book could provide the long-awaited break-through such people need; it can spare many grief and lead others to financial shrewdness that will be life-changing. Parents should give this book to their children. If everybody in Britain read it the financial atmosphere would change for the better overnight.'

Dr R.T. Kendall

What Jesus
said about
Money
and
Possessions

KEITH TONDEUR

MONARCH
BOOKS

Copyright © Keith Tondeur 1998
The right of Keith Tondeur to be identified
as author of this work has been asserted by him in
accordance with the Copyright, Designs
and Patents Act 1988

First published by Monarch Books 1998

ISBN 1 85424 418 3

Editorial Office: Monarch Books,
Broadway House, The Broadway, Crowborough,
East Sussex TN6 1HQ.

Unless otherwise stated, Scripture quotations are
taken from *The Message*. Copyright © by Eugene H Peterson,
1993, 1994,1995. Used by permission of NavPress
Publishing Group.

British Library Cataloguing Data
A catalogue record for this book is available
from the British Library.

Designed and produced for Angus Hudson Ltd by
Bookprint Creative Services
P.O. Box 827, BN21 3YJ, England
Printed in Great Britain.

This book is dedicated to my parents.

Do not be arrogant nor put your hope in wealth, which is so uncertain, but put your hope in God, who richly provides us with everything for our enjoyment. Do good, be rich in good deeds and be generous and willing to share. In this way you will lay up treasures for yourselves as a firm foundation for the coming age, so that you may take hold of the life that is truly life.

1 Timothy 6:17–19

ACKNOWLEDGEMENTS

Many people have been helpful in the production of this book, but I would particularly like to highlight two: Jacqui Smith who typed it so speedily and efficiently and Brian Keel who read it and made many valuable suggestions. Thank you both.

CONTENTS

FOREWORD

We live in a world dominated by an all consuming desire to acquire and spend money. Money, wealth, security, possessions, etc occupy so much of our time and energies. We tend to think that this is a twentieth century phenomenon but as we search the Scriptures we see Jesus, 2000 years ago, addressed the very same issues of money and wealth accumulation we face today.

As a banker working in the City of London for over 30 years and as a Christian who believes totally in the reliability and relevance of God's Word, I found Keith Tondeur's fresh interpretation of our Lord's parables on the vexed question of money and possessions so very challenging and relevant.

Conversion of our wallets and purses seems to lag well behind the conversion of our hearts and minds. Each Christian, having read this book, will be persuaded to challenge their attitude to the money and possessions of which they are but stewards and will one day be required to give an account to the Master.

In a world where there is so much need and where churches and Christian activity struggle

within limited financial resources, this book really
does encourage us to 'Seek first the Kingdom of God
... and then these things will be added unto us.'
Such a command encourages Christians to have a
light hold on the wealth and possessions of this
world, with a much firmer hold on the truths of
God's word, ensuring they are implemented in
each of our lives.

Timothy M. Green
Chief Executive of Switch Card Services Ltd.
and a Trustee of Credit Action

INTRODUCTION

WHAT JESUS SAID ABOUT MONEY AND POSSESSIONS

Having preached and spoken at many meetings over the past decade, I have come to the conclusion that Christians feel guilty if they have money and equally guilty if they don't. It is a subject that appears very personal, very private, perhaps even a little unclean. Because of this and the fact that it can too easily make us feel uncomfortable, it has become a taboo subject–it will usually only be mentioned in the context of giving.

Yet this attitude is wrong–and in fact plays straight into the hands of the enemy. Jesus had more to say about money and possessions than virtually anything else and the majority of his parables reflect these subjects to a greater or lesser degree. Given how much of our time is spent earning, spending, giving, saving or worrying about money, and given the importance we attach, especially in today's materialistic society, to having all the latest 'right-label' products, we need to see and hear exactly what Jesus is telling us.

Getting an understanding of this teaching and then applying it to our everyday lives and actions should help us find peace and contentment where now there is often fear, bewilderment and uncertainty. As you read through this book I believe you will be challenged by the strength of Jesus' words and encouraged to use money and possessions in his way. This can only bring benefit to his kingdom, to those in real need, to your neighbour, your family and even to you!

In Jesus' teaching on money and possessions there are several key themes. Sometimes there is overlap between them, but in order to concentrate the mind I have grouped the teaching into various sections. The key themes appear to me to be:

The need to sacrifice everything else for Christ and eternity.
The dangers of wealth and greed.
Debt and unconditional forgiveness.
Using money and possessions in the service of Christ.

If we can even begin to grasp what Jesus is saying here it should strengthen our commitment, deepen our trust and improve our discipleship.

PART 1

THE NEED TO SACRIFICE EVERYTHING FOR CHRIST AND ETERNITY

It is so easy to say that we put all our trust in Jesus. So often we can say it but still cling on to things which may even be good or helpful in themselves but pale into insignificance when compared with our Lord. If we really believe we are going to heaven and that we are going to be there for ever then the amount of time we spend on earth is but a blink of an eyelid. So *everything* we do on earth should be geared towards life in heaven–and this obviously includes sacrifice of temporary treasures now for eternal treasures there. Feeding the hungry, clothing the naked and leading people to Christ all add to our heavenly bank account.

The initial test
Matthew 4:1–11

The devil took him to the peak of a huge mountain. He gestured expansively, pointing out all the earth's king-doms, how glorious they were. Then he said, 'They're yours, lock, stock and barrel. Just go down on your knees and worship me and they're yours.' Jesus' refusal was curt: 'Beat it Satan.'

Immediately after John the Baptist had declared that
Jesus was the true Messiah, he was led into the
desert to be tempted. It is important to note here
that the devil did not drag Jesus there; he was in fact
taken by the Spirit. He had to be tested because he
was about to begin his ministry, preaching not only
kingdom values but also demonstrating himself as
king. And as king he had to demonstrate victory
over both the devil and the pressures and allure of
human nature. To achieve his objectives Jesus had to
face and overcome the biggest temptations available—and it is interesting that the first concerns the
lack of things and the last the temptation of many
things. At certain stages in most of our lives, albeit
to a much smaller extent, we too will be subjected to
such temptations.

I am probably the world's worst faster. I am told
that after about three days the hunger you feel dis-
appears, but I have never got that far. Medical
research also indicates that that state lasts for about
thirty days but then hunger returns as all the body's
stored resources have been completely used up. Having fasted for forty days, Jesus would have been very
hungry and could easily have 'justified' a decision to
eat again. After all, his health could suffer and his
ministry could be over before it began. It is often very
easy for us, too, to argue that decisions made,
although not Christ-like, are for the 'greater good'.
But our God is not a God of compromise. Jesus will
not put his own desires first, regardless of how desperate his situation appears. Self simply does not
come into it.

Importantly, too, Jesus did not respond to this
crisis by using his divine powers. He dealt with

the temptations as 'man'. The first temptation was to do with physical need. Rarely can there have been such temptation but Jesus wanted to demonstrate that selfishness or compromise is not the answer. When faced with difficult decisions today we can gain strength from how Jesus overcame temptation.

In the third temptation, Jesus was in fact offered every material thing–kingdoms even–if only he would bow to Satan. But the price is too high. God is to be worshipped and his will is our ultimate goal. If he is not first in all things then he is not first at all.

Get a heavenly perspective and stop worrying about the here and now
Matthew 6:19–34; Luke 12:22–34

Don't hoard treasure down here where it gets eaten by moths and corroded by rust or–worse–stolen by burglars. Stockpile treasure in heaven, where it's safe from moth and rust and burglars. It's obvious, isn't it? The place where your treasure is, is the place you will most want to be, and end up being . . . Give your entire attention to what God is doing right now and don't get worked up about what may or may not happen tomorrow.

One of the hardest things I find to focus on is the simple fact that heaven lasts for ever. Eternity is timeless. Given that that is so, the time we spend on earth is but a blink of an eyelid. When I look at it like that I can see that all my effort, thoughts and deeds should be directed to heaven. But it is so easy for everyday things to crowd in. And it is easy, too, to justify, and often get quite indignant about, the way we spend our money.

I remember being very moved by the film *Schindler's List*. This is a portrayal of a true story about a man, Oscar Schindler, who protected Jews from the Nazis. At the end of the film it showed him having to flee before the oncoming Russians. As he did so, he got to his car, looked at it and said that if he had but sold it he would have saved fifty more. Then looking at his ring he said that if he had sold that one person would have been saved. At the end of our lives I am sure we will be wondering whether we have made the right choices in the light of eternity.

We cannot take money and possessions with us. I heard of a story where a rich man insisted his pockets were full of gold coins when he was buried. At the gates of heaven he showed them in an attempt to gain entry but made no impression. He was asked, 'Why are you trying to bring pavement into heaven?' Yet on earth we often save money without really knowing why and we especially spend it on things that give at best temporary pleasure. A mere glance around my study shows that I am not the first person who should be throwing stones. Treasures on earth disappoint; they cause greed, resentment and jealousy; they lead to wrong priorities and they deflect us from caring for our Lord and our neighbours.

The reason we often concentrate on these things is fear. We simply do not trust that God will provide for us. Paul tells us: 'at the present time your plenty will supply what they need so that in turn their plenty will supply what you need' (2 Corinthians 8:14), but we scoff and inwardly think, 'Sure!' And so we concentrate on protecting and delighting ourselves, not really 'seeing' the stories of famine in our papers and on our televisions, or the homeless in our own home towns. As *The Message* tells us: we've got our blinds down. Many of us waste money and thus let both God and our neighbour down. And what is more, we often prevent God from blessing us. It is so easy to get sucked into the need to follow fashion (either to prove we are 'successful' or simply because of peer pressure–we don't want to appear to be the odd one out), but in the light of eternity how much do hemlines and hairstyles matter? (Not at all in my case!) When I used to work in the City of London it was so easy to eat regularly at expensive restaurants. Now I look forward to the occasional meal out with much more eager anticipation.

God wants to provide for us. He wants to meet all our needs. He loves us and blesses us and may well give us many of our wants as well–but he knows that some would do us harm. Do you trust him? In a world where society tells us that to be happy we have to spend, spend, spend, where the lottery invidiously breeds discontent with our lot, where a rich person is always someone who's got more than I have, *be content*. Relax, he cares for us. He will not let harm come to us. All he wants us to do is to demonstrate that we love and trust him. Just look at the colours in the sky and in the fields around you. He made you in love and wants you to let go of what you think you need and let him provide what is perfect for you.

In this consumer society, it is so easy to be preoccupied with getting and having more stuff–bigger, better, newer STUFF. Empty, soul-less stuff. We tend to think that everything of value has a price, can be bought–and that we *need* most of it. Yet the way we store up treasures says a lot about our priorities. Did you hear of the £50 note and the 50p coin talking in the bank? The £50 note said, 'I have a wonderful time. I go to expensive hotels, restaurants and health clubs. How about you?' And the 50p coin replied, 'I go to church quite a lot.'

But you can store up treasures in heaven: you can't take it with you, but you can send it on ahead. It's all to do with servanthood–not a popular word even in our churches where sadly the 'what's in it for me?' mentality can creep in. So visit a prisoner, give the hungry beggar a sandwich, buy a *Big Issue*. Put people ahead of possessions. Care for others made in the image of Christ. You will literally have for ever to rejoice. As a young Christian I ran a youth group that marked a Bible-study course for people in the Third World. About twenty new people would write in every month with the first part of the course which would be marked and sent back. About four or five every month would ask for a Bible. The children always clubbed together, often sacrificing pocket money, to ensure that anyone who asked for a Bible got one. One day we got a course from a high security prison in Africa. The writer also asked for a Bible and one was duly sent. About ten weeks later we got a reply that dramatically affected us all. It simply said this: 'I cannot thank you enough for sending the Bible. I have been reading it for hour after hour and what is more, in these last two weeks since the Bible came, six brothers have come to know Christ as their Lord and Saviour. I am not sending the next part of the course back, we are all being executed tomorrow.'

For the price of a Mars Bar each, these kids had brought six men into the kingdom. What a welcome they will get in heaven and how they'll be able to rejoice together! In the light of eternity, please please look at your priorities. I believe they should reflect the following:

• Since earth is temporary and heaven is for ever, it makes sense to store all your treasure in heaven. Do so by giving to the poor and leading others to Christ.

• I am often 'in the dark' but it is far worse for darkness to be inside me. Being generous is a clear signal that at least in one area I am moving in the light.

• God and money are two different masters and they cannot both be served. It is like trying to go both ways at a T-junction. A life determined for material prosperity will be in conflict with a life which should be devoted to God. The wise thing to do with money is to hold on to it lightly, always acknowledging that it is God's in the first place.

• Do not let money worries or the fear of the future paralyse you. God promises us the basics of life—food, clothes and shelter, and many other blessings are sure to come our way. Anxiety prevents us from helping others, weakens our faith and drains our treasures in heaven.

The parables of the hidden treasure and the pearl of great price
Matthew 13:44–46

The finder is ecstatic—what a find!

Both these parables clearly demonstrate one thing. That all the riches in the world are meaningless, especially when compared to the eternal kingdom of God. When presented with the gospel, the kingdom is offered to us as a chance of a lifetime. We need to respond decisively and be willing to give up everything for it. The fact that it exists and that we have been invited should fill us with joy, but we still have to respond and sacrifice sometimes, even the good for the best. It is a major commitment. These parables illustrate that there is a high price to pay because both finders have to get rid of all their other 'treasures' in order to possess it. There is a cost to pay–we don't get something for nothing. But what was previously important to us pales into insignificance besides heaven and besides our Lord. And so the behaviour of the finders here in selling all contrasts with the thorn-infested soil earlier in the chapter where the seed is choked by the snares of existing temporary wealth; it also encourages the disciples who have given up material things to follow Jesus.

The parable of the hidden treasure indicates that it was found during a daily routine, not by chance or by doing something extraordinary. The finder came upon it as he was doing his daily business. And one can probably come to the conclusion that he must have been doing this diligently because it is unlikely that the treasure would just be lying on the surface. We, too, by looking hard, can see God in our everyday lives. He does not just live in church on Sundays!

Every aspect of this little cameo seems so real. The joy of the man finding the treasure, the real fear that his secret will be found out and taken from him, and his eagerness to buy the field and secure the deal regardless of the cost. Each part shows the value of the treasure to the man, and Jesus is commending the man's appreciation of supreme value. One or two people have told me that they have some problems with this parable. They feel that the man deliberately conceals the hidden treasure before buying the field and thus pays an artificially low price. There are three possible answers to this:

1. It could well be that the man was within his rights. The Jewish Talmud shows that the law regarding such findings is quite clear: 'What belongs to the finder and about what must information be given? These things belong to the finder: if a man finds scattered fruit or scattered money these belong to the finder.'
2. The whole point of the parable is the finding of the treasure and the sacrificing of all else for it, just as we are called to surrender everything else for the kingdom.
3. It can be argued, as elsewhere, that Jesus is deliberately telling the story of a bit of a lad and is saying that if someone will go to all that trouble to get a treasure that does not last, then how much more should we be prepared to sacrifice in order to get the one all-important treasure. In other words, if we Christians were as committed to God as some businessmen are to making a fast buck, what a difference we could make.

In Palestine in Jesus' time it would not be that unlikely that riches could have been found in such a way. For centuries the land had been fought over and so property was insecure. Someone could well bury their treasure in the ground in the hope of retrieving it later. Death or other circumstances could prevent the collection. In fact, in Jesus' time there were professional treasure-hunters and to this day people in such areas may be hostile to archaeologists because they think they have knowledge of hidden treasure.

The pearl, meanwhile, was well known and greatly admired at that time. Simply to look at a pearl and especially to be able to touch it brought delight. Again, in the Talmud the pearl is spoken of as being beyond price. Rich people paid staggering prices for the best pearls. The merchant in the parable is a collector and a very knowledgeable person. He had probably spent years looking for the perfect pearl. Then suddenly one day he sees it. It immediately becomes his passion. He must have it. What should he do? It requires sacrifice.

In this case the merchant came upon the pearl by chance, but it was at the end of a long search for the perfect one. Equally, it is possible to get into the kingdom after a lifelong search. But again we see that the merchant had to go home and sell not just every other pearl, but also all his other assets. His other assets were not poor; it's just that they could not compare with the shining purity of this perfect pearl. To get the best he had to give up the second best. And if we want the best there will be less good things we will need to give up. Sometimes material things, sometimes the way we make money in the first place. The question we have to keep asking ourselves is what changes do we need to make to the way we live our lives now we are Christians?

We may also have to give up our comfort zones. We need to recognise our responsibilities to others. At the start of his ministry John Wesley had an income of £30 and he gave £2 away. When his income rose to much greater levels he continued to live on £28 and gave all else away. When a census of silver in England was taken, Wesley was quoted as saying, 'I have two silver spoons, one in London and one in Bristol and I am unlikely to buy any more when so many around me lack bread.'

So, both parables tell us that though there are various ways of finding, there is only one way of entering into total possession. Both the treasure finder and the pearl finder sold everything else. The kingdom of God is priceless, but it is also a free gift to all who acknowledge Jesus as Lord. We 'buy' this wonderful eternal gift by surrendering ourselves to Jesus. If we surrender everything else, it follows that risk is involved. Jesus is asking, 'Are you willing to sacrifice everything: security, comfort, possibly even your life itself, to follow me?' This willingness to risk all is the price of entry to the kingdom. We must let go of money, power and possessions, regardless of what people may think, because the kingdom of heaven is an all-surpassing gift–but this does not mean it is an easy option. In the Middle Ages there was a group of men called the *parabolani*, which means the gamblers. They literally gambled with their lives. Whenever there was trouble, risk or plague; whenever a man had to put his life at risk to help others they would be found. Certainly, it takes unconditional risk-taking to follow Jesus, and the letting go of all the things– material and otherwise–that hold us back.

The parable of the new house
Luke 14:25–30

Here Jesus tells people there is a cost to following him–they need to weigh it up before accepting him, just as they would weigh up the cost of building an expensive new house before embarking on it. God wants people he can trust, who don't put other things in the way. People who will use his vision without letting worldly things prevent it from happening. As a Christian I can no longer please myself. I must submit myself, because I want to and choose to, to my Saviour and Lord. I must also renounce the world's values. The world values power and possessions. The Christian must give away, serve and live for others. Whenever there is a conflict, Jesus must come first, at whatever cost to me personally.

The story of the lost coin
Luke 15:8–10

The money in this story could either represent the woman's savings, dowry or what she needed to pay the Temple tax. Whichever it was, it was vital to her. She would probably have lived in a small peasant's house with a low door and no windows. It will take real effort to find this coin. She must light a lamp, sweep the house and look carefully. The discovery led to much rejoicing, and she invited her neighbours to share in it. This story aptly mirrors salvation, with both the great joy of receiving it and the uncovered dust that only Jesus can really deal with.

The theme of self-sacrifice
Matthew 10:5–10; Matthew 16:24–27

Self-sacrifice is the way, my way, and finding your self, your true self.

No one should follow Jesus in order to get things out of it. (Prosperity TV evangelists please take note!) We are called to carry out our mission without seeking special rewards on earth–these will be waiting for us in heaven. In the meantime, we cannot expect to cash in blessings that we have received as a free gift from our Lord. So, being a Christian means being a good steward, accepting what comes our way. The original disciples took no money or food with them and only had one garment to wear. They demonstrated extreme poverty of wealth to contrast with the riches of their message. Sadly, greed and self-interest often get in the way.

If we do not trust that God will provide then we will not be prepared to sacrifice self as we will constantly be fearing that we haven't got enough to get by on. Or we may run the risk of sticking to 'prosperous' friends who will be able to bale us out should we hit difficulties. It is so easy to look to self and easier to look to others than it is to trust God completely. It is easier to try to find support in the false and temporary security that the world offers. It is in fact the opposite of self-aggrandisement, of demanding rights and privileges and of constantly referring to 'my' and 'mine'. Jesus has already demonstrated that he can feed thousands with a few loaves of bread and some fish. He has demonstrated that God desperately cares for each one of us and will never forsake us. We do not have to protect ourselves against every eventuality. We are to be sensible, but first and foremost we are to trust God and be generous.

Get eternal values
Luke 17:22–37

But be on your guard. Don't let the sharp edge of your expectation get dulled by parties and drinking and shopping.

Jesus is coming back! He has told us he is, so that is a fact, but we do not know when. People have been told they have been in the 'last days' for the last 2,000 years and many rumours have only led to disappointment. Whether Jesus returns in our lifetime or not, we must live as if he is imminently to return. So we should get right with God and our neighbour today. Jesus tells us that when he comes the world will be living selfishly and materialistically and will be paying little or no attention to the teachings of the Bible. So people will be amazed by the sudden judgement that will befall them. But this same day that will destroy so many will also be a day of rejoicing and redemption for God's people. So Jesus pleads with us to be ready and not to be distracted by worldly desires. Only those who are prepared to lose every material thing and even their earthly lives will survive the judgement which one day will come and finally separate us all.

PART 2

THE DANGERS OF WEALTH AND GREED

Jesus has much to say about these issues. In the West we are nearly all living in unparalleled prosperity, yet we tend to define a rich person as someone who has more money than we have and therefore think that the verses about rich people in the Bible apply to them and not to us! Sadly, this is far from the truth. It is so easy to justify our wealth but it can distance us from God and make us look down on the poor. We may blame corruption or their own ' laziness' rather than placing ourselves in their shoes. In a world that constantly bombards us with 'more, more, more' it is so easy to become greedy without even noticing it. This is precisely why Jesus personified money as 'Mammon'–another god. The following teaching shows just how dangerous 'Mammon'–can be.

The rich young ruler and the parable of the camel and the needle
Matthew 19:16–30; Mark 10:17–31; Luke 18:18–30

Do you have any idea how difficult it is for the rich to enter God's kingdom? . . . but anyone who sacrifices home, family, friends–whatever–because of me will get it back a hundred times over, not to mention the considerable bonus of eternal life.

There is a certain amount of debate among scholars as to whether the meeting with the rich young ruler was a real-life encounter or part of the parable of the camel and the eye of the needle. Whichever you believe, it is clear that Jesus has strong words to say about those who are obsessed by acquiring or maintaining wealth.

The man who comes to Jesus is looking for eternal life. He wants happiness, to feel satisfied and be at peace with God, but the very way he asks the question, 'What must I do' shows that he has no understanding of what eternal life is all about. And as riches and power often go hand in hand, it is a danger to us all. We cannot manipulate God. We cannot use our resources to bully, cajole or even persuade God, and nor should we to our fellow men and women.

Rich people tend to have a habit of getting their own way, and then accepting that as how it should be. But despite his wealth the rich man knew there was something more. He might have felt secure about today, but he was worried about the future. In his muddled thinking he seemed to think he could open up a credit account with God. He only had to do a few things now to secure him eternal life in the future.

Having been asked the question, Jesus answers the young man in similar fashion by telling him to keep the commandments. In particular, Jesus mentions those that relate to our fellow citizens. They refer to individual and personal relationships. Jesus also puts one commandment last, which would normally have come earlier, almost as if he wanted to emphasise it. It is to love your neighbour as yourself.

Either with the blind self-confidence of youth or the false security that riches bring, the young ruler felt confident that he had done it all. He had kept the law in all aspects—even though he knew there was something missing. So Jesus decided to challenge him and told him to 'go sell your possessions. Give everything to the poor.' Then, and only then, could he follow Jesus and, by implication, have eternal life. For many this can touch the heart of the commandments, because it is so easy to try and find security in one's possessions that they become more important than anything else. The rich young ruler could not surrender his possessions and put God first because, when the chips were down, they had pride of place.

To make things easier for us to grasp, it may well be worth looking at this parable as told in the Gospel to the Hebrews which was excluded from the New Testament. It reads: 'Go and sell all you own and distribute it to the poor and come and follow me.' But the rich man began to scratch his head because this displeased him. And the Lord said to him, 'How can you say you have kept the Law and the Prophets? For it is written in the Law: "You shall love your neighbour as yourself", but many of your fellow-believers are clad in filth, dying of hunger and yet your house is full of many good things and nothing goes out of it to them.'

This helps to unlock the whole point that Jesus is making. Legally the young man may have kept the Law, but spiritually he was in the wrong because of his selfish behaviour. Even when challenged by Jesus he still could not see that he had done anything wrong. Giving away everything would have been hard in those times. It is equally difficult today when others judge us by what we own. Having seems more important than being. In this case the young man was so encumbered by his possessions, so weighed down, that the only way he could be released was for him to give them all away. If we look at our possessions and view them as merely for our benefit, we need to ask God to work in our lives. God only tells people who hold possessions purely for themselves to give them away. To others who see them as a means of helping others in distress they are a blessing. God is likely to increase the possessions in such cases because the recipients are demonstrating the heart of God and they can be trusted to be his 'wallets' on earth.

Eternal life cannot be bought with money, and everything of value does not have a price tag on it. The rich cannot buy their way into heaven in the same way that they can buy whatever they want on earth. The rich young ruler turned away extremely upset. He could not accept the ultimate challenge because at the end of the day the many things he possessed mattered more than anything else. Possessions came before people and he thought of himself before considering others. Anyone doing this is rejecting Jesus. God can work the wonders of conversion in anyone, even the rich. Jesus promises us that whoever gives up everything to follow him will receive a much greater reward. However, riches do make it a lot harder to follow Jesus, for a variety of reasons. These include:

• Riches encourage a sense of false self-security. If you own more than sufficient you think you can cope with anything that arises and, if necessary, buy yourself out of trouble.

• Riches imply that anything of value can be bought. Not just material things but also happiness and the elimination of sadness. If you feel you can do that and manage your own life so effectively, why do you need God? Obviously this will eventually prove to be false, as an increasing number of testimonies from lottery winners indicate, as peace of mind eludes or illness strikes or death approaches. But there is still always this danger of false independence that removes the need for God.

• Riches tend to make you selfish. Enough never seems to be enough. Furthermore, once a little luxury has been enjoyed you really begin to fear that some day this will be lost. So life becomes a constant struggle to keep the things you have. On Credit Action's debt helpline we hear from people who lack things, but equally we hear from a lot of people who are worrying about losing things which, if they had never had in the first place they never would have missed! So riches can make people hoard even more rather than be increasingly generous as they search for that all-elusive security. Riches can make people forget 'that they lose what they keep and gain what they gave away'.

• Riches are ties to earth rather than heaven. If our treasures are to be found on earth we will spend little or no time thinking about eternity. Riches can make you feel immortal, and visible things can so ensnare us that we forget the unseen. This is disastrous because the visible is temporary but the unseen can be eternal.

Despite all this, God can still break through. Zacchaeus was one of the richest men around, as were Joseph of Arimathea and Nicodemus. It is not those that have riches that are shut out. Indeed, people with riches often close the door themselves. Having money is not a sin, but it is a real danger–and it is only self-denial that will keep the door wide open.

These passages are not sent to condemn but certainly they can warn us. Most of us in the West are rich by worldly standards and, to some degree, will be influenced by advertising, our fellow men and women, and our culture. When we think of buying something, we need to ask God about it just as we ask him about every other aspect of our lives. He loves us and wants us to enjoy many blessings. Sometimes these will be in the form of giving instead of receiving. Honouring him, even the richest can 'pass through the eye of a needle'.

The story of the greedy farmhands
Matthew 21:33–44; Mark 12:1–9; Luke 20:9–16

'When the farmhands saw the son arrive they rubbed their hands in greed. "This is the heir! Let's kill him and have it all for ourselves." They grabbed him, threw him out and killed him. Now, when the owner of the vineyard arrives home from his trip what do you think he'll do to the farmhands?' 'He'll kill them–a rotten bunch and good riddance,' they answered. 'Then he'll assign the vineyard to farmhands who will hand over the profits when it's time.'

This is one of the few full-length parables that is to be found in all three synoptic Gospels, which must reflect the impact that it made when Jesus told it. As usual, there are various themes that run through the story, but in this parable, as we shall see, every detail has a meaning.

Jesus was describing a situation which was common in his day. Palestine was a much fought over land and absentee landlords were numerous. It was very tempting, if one was wealthy, to rent out the land you owned and go and live in a safer country. When this happened, rent would be collected either in terms of cash or in terms of a percentage of the crop gathered. This was always a difficult time because there was unrest and many tenants found reason not to pay the rent and would use violence if necessary in an attempt to gain ownership of land that was not theirs.

It is now important to look at what Jesus is really saying so some of the meanings become clearer. The vineyard represents the people of Israel, the farmer is God. The farmhands represent the priests and Pharisees who have imposed their laws on Israel, and the badly treated servants represent the prophets of God who have often been ignored and even martyred. The son is Jesus himself. So the parable shows God's patience with his people, their ongoing rejection of him, the sending of his only son and his being put to death and finally the triumph of God and the discomfort of all those who had rejected him. The parable thus demonstrates how God has cared for Israel. The vineyard was planted–it was converted from a wilderness. It was fenced to protect it from outside attack, a winepress was installed which would enable the grapes to be pressed effectively and a watchtower was built which would enable people to have both advanced warning of any danger but also shelter. Everything that could have been done had been done, and so the vineyard should have been highly fruitful.

Everything, at a deeper level, had been done for Israel so that they would recognise and honour Jesus as the Son of God. They failed completely. And this raises questions about us and the way we live. We have so many privileges. We have nice houses, live in a 'Christian' country with freedom of worship, good health and education systems. How are we using our privileges today? Are we acknowledging who has given them to us and thanking him for them?

The parable also emphasises the fact that we can all make choices. God has given us the opportunity of doing good or evil, of following him or of following selfish desires. In this parable, as soon as the farmer had got the vineyard in perfect condition, he left. The farmhands had freedom to run the vineyard their way. There was no interference. They were free men. The only thing they had to do was to pay a percentage of the fruit they produced as rent. The remainder of the produce was available to them. The farmhands could have chosen to be good stewards, as we all can today, but they failed to show respect to the farmer and tried to claim the property for themselves. As they did so, the initial rebellion of beating a servant up continued to build until they killed another servant and then the farmer's own son. This is how easy it is for a smallish sin to lead to worse and worse. There is no indication that these farmhands were bad people. They had not been idle. In fact, it looks as if they had worked hard in that they were unwilling to share their profits with the farmer. Almost certainly they will have been justifying their own positions. For example, most vines take at least five years to reach full maturity and so in the early years profits may have been low. Perhaps they felt that they could not 'afford' to give their master the first fruits (how often we hear that today!).

In the parable the farmer deals openly with the

farmhands. He had been good to them and entered into a legal arrangement. So initially he only felt he needed to send one servant as no trouble was expected. The owner had to make arrangements for the rent to be collected because if he failed to do so for a number of years the farmhands could claim possession for themselves. But the servant was not only sent away empty handed, he was given a good beating as well. Whether this was because the servant refused to leave without the rent, because the vineyard had little profit or because it was a warning to the farmer not to send anyone again is open to conjecture. Again, we do not know whether the next servant was sent immediately or whether he went at the following harvest in the hope that the farmhands' attitude may have softened because of a better harvest. In any event, they refused to pay at least three more times and at this stage the idea must have been growing that, if they could keep this up for a bit longer they could actually gain ownership of the vineyard. In their self-centred worlds they saw themselves more as masters than servants. But the farmer (God) stands in the way of their plans and every time a messenger comes it reminds them of the true situation.

The farmer is left with but one option, short of going himself. He must send someone with more authority than a servant, someone with the power and prestige to get things sorted out. The only candidate is his son. When he arrives it appears as if the farmhands make an instantaneous decision to kill him, although they may well have talked about it before. They would know that, as the farmer's only son, he would be heir to the estate. They reason that if they kill him eventually the vineyard will become theirs. By killing him they would not have to pay rent for the fourth time and therefore would be able to establish their claim for legal possession. But the fact that the rent collector was the heir's only son may have sparked a new idea. They may have assumed that the original owner had already died and that the son was now the rightful owner. If he died the vineyard would pass to them as they had the prior claim on the vineyard and it would be regarded as ownerless property. Whatever they thought, it was foolish and short-sighted because the farmer was not dead and was bound to act once they killed his son.

In any event, they decided to act so they threw the son out of the vineyard and killed him (presumably far enough away from the vineyard to look as if they were unconnected with his death). But even in killing the heir the farmhands have not won. All of them eventually have to deal with the farmer, just as we all have to deal with God. And it is at this very point that Jesus stops and turns to his audience and asks them what the farmer should do. They condemn themselves with their own lips, although by then it is obvious what the answer will be. The farmer will have the farmhands destroyed, either by some form of armed attack or by bringing them to trial for murder, and the vineyard will be given to new tenants who will behave respectfully, acknowledging the rightful owner and giving him what is his.

This parable clearly demonstrates God's patience towards us and also his sacrificial love. He provides a well-tended and bountiful living place and sends reminder after reminder about himself with such persistence that we wonder at his calmness. He even sends his only Son, knowing that we will kill him because of our selfish ways. He is a God of patience, but also one of power and purpose. He wants us to acknowledge what he has done for us so we can be redeemed.

So why did the farmhands reject the patience of God? They clearly knew how they should behave. They knew the difference between right and wrong, between good and evil. But they were selfish. They did not want to be merely good stewards. They wanted to possess everything: the fruit and the profits and the vineyard itself. They wanted to look and feel important.

Are we different from the farmhands? As servants we want to produce good fruit and maximum 'profit'– but for the kingdom. We too have freedom of choice. Freedom to do right or wrong, freedom to double our talents or to bury them. We are not free to select our birth or our 'vineyard', but we are free to do the best we can or alternatively compare our lot unfavourably with others. But we also have responsibilities to bear good fruit so it reflects well on our master. We have great privileges but we also have obligations–none of which is beyond our ability to cope with.

Being challenged about how we live, and especially acknowledging that everything is God's, hit home hard when Jesus first taught it and it hits equally hard today. It feels as if a raw nerve has been touched whenever our use of money, possessions, lifestyle or comfort zone is challenged. Our initial reaction is nearly always one of wanting to shoot the messenger. But if we first stop and let God work in our hearts then he will help us to break through and break free. As from today, let him own 'your' money and possessions. He will not let you down!

The parable of the wedding banquet
Matthew 22:1–10; Luke 14:12–24

'Come to the Feast.' But they only shrugged their shoulders and went off, one to weed his garden, another to work in his shop.

This is a story about a man who prepares a great feast. In Palestine it would be a normal occurrence. A date would be fixed some time in the future but not the exact time. On the day in question the honoured guests were actually summoned by servants, while the others either couldn't believe they'd been invited so got there early so they didn't miss anything or arrived at the last minute and made a show of how important they were.

So the parable describes the banquet being ready and the already invited guests are summoned to attend. But one after another they made their excuses. *The Message* says that one went to weed his garden, another to attend to his shop. The former shows a trivial excuse–something that could be done at any time and was therefore a calculated insult to the king. The latter too is appropriate for today, as this man was too busy with his job to spend time with the king. The NIV says that one had gone to inspect a field he had recently purchased. Presumably he had not bought this unseen and so wanted to bask in the glory of his assets: 'It's mine at last!' Another had bought some oxen and it was imperative that he tried them out immediately. Again, it is unlikely he would have bought them untested. But he wanted them to set to work straight away, probably to ensure they maximised profits. He was probably financially 'successful', but financial 'success' can often impede spiritual growth.

In the Middle East, not to provide good hospitality is an affront, but to refuse such hospitality is a deliberate insult. So the king determined to fill the empty places and sent out to the poor and needy to attend. At one level, then, Jesus is giving advice about how to choose guests you wish to entertain. Having already approved humility (not a common trait of a Pharisee), he then further stretched credulity by suggesting that the people invited should not just be the socially acceptable but should include the poor and needy– those who could never return the favour.

Jesus liked feasts. He came eating and drinking (Matthew 11:19) and he enjoyed the pleasures of life. How the outcasts would have enjoyed the feast that day! Lame beggars jostling with others with their crutches, blind ones staggering into others and the dumb mumbling incoherently but showing their obvious joy at this unexpected treat. Feeding the fellow rich will result in an invite back–an earthly reward. We should be reaching out to all we come across in need and leave any question of recompense up to God, happy in the knowledge that we are doing his will.

Jesus showed how easy it is for our own desires and even the busyness of day-to-day living to prevent us from getting close to him. As his invitation has eternal importance we should value it above all else. Certainly we should not allow possessions to get in the way.

At a deeper level, those originally invited were the Jews. They were the chosen people. All through their history they had been waiting for the Messiah. What is more, the idea of a great banquet was well established. Jews believed that when the Messiah came there would be a great banquet for all those present. This is confirmed by various Old Testament references, especially Isaiah 25:6–9 which refers to a great banquet for all people. However, the Jews came arrogantly to believe that it would only apply to them. Thus, the rejection of the invitation by the Jews opened the door for all who would believe.

Similarly, God does not turn to the poor because he loathes the rich. It is usually because God calls the poor to the banquet as well that the rich stay away. The rich, the poor, the good, the bad–all are sinners. So the rich are only excluded when they show by their actions that they reject the salvation which is available for all. The better-off can feel uncomfortable or even scandalised by the concern Jesus shows for the poor. It is so easy for us to shrug our shoulders when we hear of needs or things we should support because we have too many other important things to do. We can easily feel relatively good about ourselves, feel that we have never committed any major crime and should therefore automatically be able to get into heaven. Some, while even not responding to the message themselves, will be outraged when they see people they look down on being invited in. In Jesus' audience there would have been both rich and poor. The rich just knew that they would be going as long as it was sufficiently important and exclusive and the host was well known. They can see no reason why they should not be there. But perhaps they have become blasé or too self-important. And, as Jesus gives out the excuses in the parables, they secretly recognise that they have given such excuses themselves. Not being prepared to admit this, of course, they first seethe away in silent resentment. They want to be able to choose for themselves whether or not to attend.

On the other hand, the poor in the audience would feel hungry just at the thought of a banquet. Of course they would secretly love to be invited, but what hope do they have? After all, these sorts of things only happen in fairy tales, don't they? Not any more they don't! The rich would be too preoccupied with their money and businesses to perceive the enormity of the invitation. Jesus' message was in reality too simple for them fully to understand. But again, here we have a message of grace–offering an invitation to those who did not expect it or deserve it. Not only are they invited, they are almost pulled into the banqueting hall.

Before we close this section, look again at the excuses offered. The buying of a field and the need to go and see it implies that this possession is more important than the relationship with the king. The man who bought the oxen is obsessed with new things. Many of us can get obsessed with new things to such an extent that everything else is driven from our minds. People can start coming to church and they won't miss a meeting for months and suddenly they are not there any more. Something new has come into their lives. Whereas we should not be afraid of the new, we also need the permanence of God.

All the reasons given were to some extent valid. Gardens do need weeding and businesses do need working at. One of the difficulties we, as Christians, face, is that it is good things that can come between us and Jesus. If the temptation was awful it would be much easier to reject it. We must not let the good get in the way of the best–our loving the Lord Jesus. Let us unreservedly accept his generous invitation today.

The parable of the greedy farmer (or rich fool)
Luke 12:13–21

*Just then God showed up and said, 'Fool. Tonight you die.
And your barnful of goods, who gets it?' This is what
happens when you fill your barn with self and not with
God. Be generous. Give to the poor. Get yourself a bank
that can't go bankrupt, a bank in heaven far from bank-
robbers, safe from embezzlers, a bank you can bank on.*

This parable is timeless and yet probably more relevant today than at any other time. It is the story of a
man who thinks life is a doddle. Everything smells of
roses. Everything he touches turns to gold. He thinks
of himself as immortal and then he suddenly dies.

The background to this parable is that of a younger
brother asking Jesus to intervene and tell his elder
brother to give him a fairer share of the family inheritance. Jewish law on this subject was quite clear,
however. The eldest got two-thirds and one-third
was divided between the other sons. The younger
brother undoubtedly knew this law well enough, he
just wanted a larger share. He coveted more and he
wanted it now. In many cases, in fact, the elder
brother would keep the inheritance undivided to
make it more economically viable and ensure his
brothers were well looked after. As Psalm 133 says,
'How good it is when brothers dwell in unity.'

Jesus refuses to intervene in the dispute, partly
because he feels unqualified to do so as it is a family
matter, but also because he is opposed to the greedy
nature which underlies the request for help. It is precisely this hidden reason behind the request that leads
Jesus to telling this parable, which is of such relevance

to us all. This story is, in fact, told again in shortened
form in Thomas 63:

> There was a rich man who had much money. He said, 'I
> shall put my money to use so that I may sow, reap, plant
> and fill my storehouse with produce, with the result that I
> shall lack nothing.' Such were his intentions. And that
> night he died. Let him who has ears fear.

The parable clearly shows Jesus' strong disapproval of
such selfish motives. He gives a clear warning about
the desire for more by implying that the younger
brother will not have his problems solved by getting
more. (Incidentally, this is very similar to people who
overspend today and believe an immediate loan will
resolve all their problems!) Just because people have
more does not mean that their lives will be better. The
lifestyle of a rich person can in itself cause problems
such as loneliness and isolation. But when someone
who has been living from hand to mouth suddenly
sees prosperity, they have a critical decision to make.
Will they mature and take it in their stride or will they
spend rashly on themselves? Possessions cost time,
money and effort. Too many and you may well feel
that they possess you! Having money brings responsibility, both in spending and giving.

Here the rich man has no one close to him. He has no
one close enough to him to share the dilemma. Wealth
can easily bring this form of isolation. His money
basically buys him a vacuum to live in 'splendid isolation'. Living without considering others is bound to
lead to a warped sense of perspective. So the rich
man's main interest is clear—himself. He refers to no
one, neither God nor man. He just thinks of 'terrific
crops', 'take it easy' and 'have the time of your life'. He

never looks beyond himself. He never looks beyond
the here and now. He never looks beyond the world.

It is important to remember that Jesus does not
condemn all wealth. Yes, he told the rich young
man to sell everything but that was an individual
instruction rather than a general command. But he
does issue strong warnings about the negative impact
that 'many things' can do to one's character. Jesus had
little earthly wealth and did not desire it. He was not
envious of those with more than him. In fact he spoke
with pity because he knew that often it is important to
surrender some worldly goods for the sake of the
eternal kingdom. Today, especially, his non-materia-
listic attitudes haunt our greedy ways and convict us
accordingly. I believe many of us will radically have
to alter the way we use 'our' money if we want to see
genuine revival. After all, a follower of Jesus should
have a true sense of values, recognising that real life is
not measured by possessions. It only needs God to
take away someone's life to make it obvious that
ultimately possessions are of no value to them.

So someone may have a large bank balance, but if
they disregard God and their fellowmen and women
they are poor, not rich. They are as foolish as they are
short-sighted. They may have prepared for their own
immediate comfort, but failed to prepare for their own
eternal destiny. If only they had been generous to
others they could have stored up a lasting treasure in
heaven. Possessions are superficial and desire for them
steers people away from what is really important.

It is interesting to note that the man is rich at the
beginning of the story. He just had nowhere to store
his ever-increasing supply of goods. He assumed his
wealth would last, the problem was simply what to

do with it. It appears as if he has come by his wealth honestly. His farm was successful but he does not appear to cheat on others. Similarly, he was not a miser as he was planning to retire and have the good things of life. In fact, he seemed practical and had all the makings of a successful businessman. As his farm expanded he needed bigger barns (a reflection of some churches' philosophy today!) and he moved forward confidently. He would be somebody important today–a key player. But Jesus called him a fool–not because of his success but because of his wrong priorities. As Christians we are called to be in the world but not of it. We must not allow our things to dominate our lives. But the rich man in this parable was so inward looking and so concerned about 'his' goods that he and they became one and the same thing. He was absorbed with what he owned. And his self-centredness just grew and grew.

The rich fool is given to us by Jesus as a warning. He concentrated on trivial things while forgetting the essential; it is so easy for us to do the same. First, he remembered himself. Never have so many 'I's, 'my's and 'mine's been put together in such a small number of words. As good stewards, by acknowledging that all is God's we should be eliminating the words 'I' and 'my'. Go on and try it, it's very hard to do for long! Am 'I' at the centre of 'my' world?

Somehow the rich fool forgot God who made the soil fertile and the crops grow under the sun. He needed rain, light, heat, but the crops were 'mine'. Equally, if his crops were so big he needed more barns it is highly unlikely he would have ploughed, sowed, reaped and built by himself. Wealth is always a product of ideas, land and hard work–and they are not all carried out by the same person. So, to a greater or lesser degree, the rich man will have become affluent because of others, but he never once thought about others. 'Self' is the rudest four-letter word in the English language!

Then the rich man thought of the world to such an extent that to him it was all that mattered. He believed that if only he could amass sufficient things he would be happy and secure. But it will not work. It is like the Jewish saying, 'Who so craves wealth is like a man who drinks sea water. The more he drinks the more he increases his thirst and he ceases not to drink until he perishes.' Equally, it is believed that Jesus said, 'The world is a bridge. The wise man will pass over it but will not build his house upon it.' By this he means that, although this world has importance, it is but a stepping-stone to another and far superior world. Forget that and you forget the real meaning of living here. It is sheer stupidity that drives people to burn themselves out and suffer breakdowns in the constant pursuit of more things. The tragedy for people like the rich fool is that the sudden death of their body confirms that their soul has died already. In the amassing of things I believe you can die as you live. The rich man's money and possessions had robbed him of ideals and friendships which are real treasures. When death occurs the thin line between self and one's possessions becomes a gulf.

The fact that the rich man's death came at precisely the height of his material prosperity only adds to the story. We measure success by how much people have and what they earn. We search for immortality with our personalised number plates. We dare not let them go, but they have not bought us peace. The more labour-saving devices we have the busier we seem to get. The more things we possess the more anxious and dissatisfied we become. Whatever we want, we want more and we want something bigger and better than before and certainly better than our next-door neighbour's. We are moving so fast that we do not stop and question whether this is progress or actually more damaging to us and our society. Sadly, there have been plenty of lives cut short that demonstrate that the mere accumulation of things with no concern for others is suicidal. Materialism in our society is an excuse we use for our own self-centred conduct. Our characters and generosity need to grow in line with our acquisitions or else the shallowness of our lives will be clearly visible.

At this point we should recall that this parable is all about the accumulation of goods that are well surplus to requirements. The rich man already had more than enough for his needs. It is not something to apply to those struggling to cope on a day-by-day basis. But it does demonstrate that dreams of an abundant life through an accumulation of surplus simply will not work. In our society today we have an unstoppable demand for an ever-increasing standard of living. The belief that always having more almost as a matter of right is also with us. With the world's natural resources dwindling, the population continuing to grow rapidly and this pressure for more increasing, Jesus' message has to be urgently regarded. We all need to avoid greed. It is not just about government or company irresponsibility. It is down to individual responsibility and it starts with me.

You see, the rich man forgot his neighbours. There would certainly have been many in the locality who would probably have been desperate for just a tiny amount of his surplus. His idea of happiness was to please himself. He had not yet matured enough to learn that true enjoyment comes from being at peace–by making God and others happy. Selfishness cannot bring true enjoyment. J.M. Barrie expressed it like this: 'Those who bring sunshine into the lives of others cannot keep it from their own.' But the rich man, when asking, 'What can I do?' did not consider the sick, the hungry and the naked. They never came into his thinking. In certain Christian circles, and in the selfishness of 'prosperity' teaching, there can be a tendency to accumulate riches, justify it and so care for neighbours only reluctantly.

Secondly, the rich man forgot time. He thought life would just continue as it was. We all have very limited time and Jesus warns us of this not to depress or frighten us, but to challenge us to prepare properly for a higher and permanent world. On death a soul will travel one way, but possessions stay behind. Only 'inward' treasure can be carried with you. Have we really chosen between mundane temporary treasure and God's eternal blessings? It is hard to take this on board. At times I think I am making progress and then believe there is still so much I should do. Do I have the courage to fully obey? What impact will it have in my world which can still be so cluttered with things? Yet when death comes no amount of goods, however well looked after or carefully stored, will be of any help. God's timing is not our timing. It is so easy to make assumptions about the future (and everyone who uses credit does that!) and think we'll put something right later on. But with death everything stops there and then. Because the rich man had focused exclusively on increasing his wealth to the exclusion of all else, he has nothing to take forward with him. And his suddenly enforced silence leaves us to answer individually for ourselves.

Ultimately, the rich man forgot the very God that had created him. Look at James 4:13–15–'And now I have a word for you who brashly announce, "Today–at the latest tomorrow–we're off to such a city for the year. We're going to start a business and make a lot of money." You don't know the first thing about tomorrow. You're nothing but a wisp of fog catching a brief bit of sun before disappearing. Instead make it a habit to say, "If the master wills it and we're still alive we'll do this or that."' The rich man had left out the most important factor of all. Real treasure involves helping others, but especially finding Jesus whose love for us forgives us our sins, a treasure which can compare with nothing. In the end, by failing to grow rich towards God, he failed even to gather any wealth for himself.

You can grow rich towards God by letting things go and giving to others. The rich fool forgot that a man is what he is, not what he has. Society today tries to tell us that 'having' is more important than 'being'. Death cannot take away kindnesses to others or others being brought into the kingdom. It is a subject that we all don't like to think about, including many Christians. We need to remember what the Spanish proverb tells us: 'There are no pockets in a shroud.' We are not masters of our own destiny. We cannot rationalise our future with certainty. Things are not to be stored away. They are to be used to benefit relationships.

And so Jesus clearly tells us that the supreme aim in life is not the acquisition of temporary things but the development of a generous character that will find favour with both God and our needy fellow men and women.

The parable of the rich man and Lazarus
Luke 16:19–31

There was once a rich man, expensively dressed in the latest fashion, wasting his days in conspicuous consumption. He died . . . Abraham said, 'Remember that in your lifetime you got the good things and Lazarus the bad things. It's not like that here.'

The condemnation of greatly differentiating wealth, as expressed here, is one of the most pertinent things we can draw from Jesus' ministry. Various Church fathers have expressed it through time thus: Augustine–'To succour the needy is justice'; Ambrose–'You are not giving the poor person the gift of a part of what is yours. You are returning to him something of what is his'; Chrysostom–'Do not say, "I am spending what is mine." It is not actually yours. It is someone else's'; Basil–'It is the hungry ones' bread you keep, the needy ones' money that you have saved'; Jerome–'All riches originally derive from injustice.'

The words above are enough to make me feel very uneasy for a start! But Jesus constantly criticised unfeeling wealth and encouraged the often uncomplaining poor. He could not believe that people blessed with plenty could ignore the cries of the hurting. It is so easy to judge others; to believe that I am not like that, not like the Pharisees. I can read of medieval feasts and feel disgusted at the contrast between the gluttony inside the castle and the hunger outside. But in 1,000 years time will people look at our society, see the enormous gap between rich and poor and wonder how we dared call ourselves Christians? As I started to write this book I came to a shuddering stop at this story. For years I have felt that the rich man (Dives) was an uncaring and nasty piece of work who deserved his eventual fate. But as I began to unpack it my preconceptions were totally eroded. For in many ways this man was kinder to the poor than I am. Do I have a beggar at my table every day? Do I give him what's left over? Am I living out what I read in God's word, what I know Jesus said, what I even teach and write about? Lord help me to see and to act.

This is the only parable in which a character is given a proper name. 'Lazarus' is the Greek name for the Hebrew 'Eleazar' which means 'God is my help'. Jesus may well have been emphasising that even if others let the poor down, God will never forsake them. It also means that everyone is special to God and is known by name. The audience would have expected the rich man to have a name and the poor man to be anonymous, but the opposite is the case. The beggar was really special to God.

Jesus begins by showing the chasm that there is between the way the two men lived; a chasm that the rich man could cross if he chose to. The rich man was clothed in all the latest 'designer-label' luxury fashion which would have been bought at great cost. The purple and fine linen would have been imported from Egypt or India, and just wearing them shouted out 'I am something special'—just like today's personalised car number plates. The rich man also feasted magnificently every day. It is important to stress the 'every'. All of us like enjoyment, good food, etc. It is part of the many blessings that God bestows upon us. But to feast like that all the time just shows selfishness and gluttony, especially when there are starving on our doorsteps. The rich man is not criticised so much for his waste as he is for his lack of concern for others. He just enjoyed his wealth. He could afford to live like that and justified his actions accordingly. (Wesley said 'afford' was the word he hated most in the English language.) So he coasts along, like the rich man with his barns, unaware of his impending eternal fate.

But it is important to note that Jesus has not condemned the rich man as an unscrupulous rogue. There is no indication of dishonesty or meanness. The fact that a beggar was being brought to his table daily implies that he was, to a degree, looking after him. A beggar would only return (or be returned) to somewhere where he would at least be fed. So the rich man probably considered himself as kind and charitable in feeding the beggar the scraps from his table. After all, which of his neighbours did the same? But he did nothing to help Lazarus' position improve. He allowed the status quo, and thereby the injustice, to continue. Lazarus lived a life in sharp contrast to the well–fed and contented rich man. He has to be carried daily to the rich man's house. This does not have to mean that he was paralysed, just that he was poor and hungry. His rags did not decently cover his body, which was covered in ulcers, and he was so weak that he did not have the strength to drive off the semi-wild dogs that roamed the streets. He would sit beneath the table and wait for food. This could either be the 'crumbs' which fell by accident and would normally have been eaten by the dogs, or pieces of bread which were used to wipe and clean one's hands (no knives or forks in those days remember) before being thrown to the floor. And Lazarus considered himself lucky!

Before we move on to the second part of the story, let us look at this contrast again because it stares out at

us in our world today too. The rich man appears charitable but his 'love' and 'concern' for Lazarus were so
negligible they almost cause indignation. He saw
Lazarus every day, but he never *saw* him once. There
was no real compassion–his hungry, ulcerated body
left him unmoved. He didn't feel that he must do something about it. It was just part of life and it was his good
fortune that he was where he was. He remained selfish;
his crime was not that he was rich, for that was his
opportunity. It was his self-centredness that caused
offence. Instinctively he would have known that love
and compassion were the 'best' things on earth but the
lure of riches blinded him to the truth he once would
have known. Tragic circumstances had forced Lazarus
to be as he was. Did the rich man ever stop and think, 'I
could have been born into such a situation. Life could
have been that hard for me. There but for the grace of
God go I'? And so his potential for good was replaced
by inward-looking greed.

If the rich man had fed Lazarus properly, washed
and clothed him, it would have helped somewhat. But
true charity is more than putting a copper in a collection box or buying a *Big Issue* once. It must be neither
occasional or superficial. It should lead to non-
acceptance of the contrast between rich and poor,
between the powerful and the powerless. Feeding the
needy scraps belittles us, them and God. It is so easy to
be like the rich man and justify our position. Lazarus
was not claimed by Jesus to be 'good'. He was just poor.
The rich man could not say, 'Well, if only I'd known he
was good I would have done more to help him.' So
there are no religious undertones in this message. It is
about the gulf between rich and poor, between heaven
and earth. And it is about the real danger of just

mixing with a certain class of person (your own) and failing to enter into dialogue with the really hurting.

The turning point of the story comes with the death of both men. They suffer a radical reversal of fortunes, demonstrated by the fact that they are mentioned in reverse order. To be in the 'lap of Abraham' describes paradise or heaven. The fact that Lazarus is so close to Abraham indicates he is being honoured. The rich man died. His burial is mentioned probably because it had much ritual and 'show' and was the last time that his wealth could be spent on himself. But he found himself in hell, where he 'looked up' and saw Lazarus and realised his true position. It is as if there has been a complete reversal of the earlier picture on earth. Lazarus is now 'rich' in companionship and honour, whereas the rich man desperately needs some help–even a drop of water–from Lazarus.

It was common Jewish and early Christian belief that heaven and hell were in sight of one another as a constant reminder of how we have chosen to live our lives on earth. And in this particular parable Abraham reminds the rich man that he had already received his good things on earth. At that time he had thought that fine clothes and rich food were 'good'. Now he painfully began to realise what 'good' really meant. Worse still, Abraham states that no one can cross the great chasm between heaven and hell. It is a chasm that the rich man had dug by himself while on earth. It is too easy for us to do the same. We ignore the needs of our fellow men and women, become more selfish and more inflexible, and as we do so we make the chasm deeper and harder for us to fill back in. Our compassion should direct our wealth rather than be squashed by it.

So in hell the rich man cries out for mercy, to

Abraham—whom he acknowledges as 'Father'. He asks him to send Lazarus to aid him. Even then he primarily considers Lazarus as someone who is inferior and should tend to his needs. When had he ever given a moment's thought to the needs of Lazarus on earth? But it was too late. Lazarus could not have helped even if he had wanted to.

Interestingly, at this stage the parable clearly shows things about the afterlife. First, identity still remains. The rich man and Lazarus were who they were and their personalities along with them. We need to remember that we take what we are with us when we die. Secondly, memory clearly remains. Looking back at the pain I have caused others will be hard to endure but will also deepen my praise for my redeemer who has forgiven me so much. And wonderfully, memory remains. We will meet again all those we loved but have lost or left behind for a moment on earth.

One of the points of the parable is that if someone gets what they want they will end up paying the price for it. The rich man chose worldly things—now he was paying the price. On the other hand, Lazarus, as his name shows, had to rely on God for help. We seem to be able to purchase everything in the world for a price—except peace of mind and eternal life which are gifts of God free for us if we choose them. Just as the devil tempted Jesus with everything, so we have this choice too. Eternity can bring both compensation and reward for how we have lived on earth. But it can also bring eternal retribution. And death fixes the fate of someone for ever.

Having given up on himself, the rich man then asks Abraham at least to help others like him on earth who do not realise what they are doing—especially his brothers. His thought is that if they knew their selfish lifestyle was leading them straight to hell, then, if something miraculous happened, like somebody rising from the dead, they would change their ways. This, of course, would lead to salvation by good deeds, however amazingly done. They would also definitely know that they would be rewarded for their behaviour. Their motives would be all wrong.

The rich man is saying that these people were living under a handicap. They hadn't been warned sufficiently that unless they mended their ways they were hellbound. If only he'd known he never would have lived so selfishly. But he had been given ample warning, and we have actually got this very parable to warn us, but how much difference does it make to our everyday actions? We constantly want bigger signs, more impressive wonders, more individual 'zaps' to make us feel good about ourselves. Even in our faith there can be so much self-centredness. When do we put ourselves in the shoes of Lazarus–the lost, hungry, lonely and hurting? When do we, as in the wonderful words of Johnny Markin, 'See with your eyes'? And then when do we do something about it? We have Jesus' word. We have his Spirit living within us. If we do not see how we should live we must be blind indeed. There should be no 'Lazarus' that I see and feel unmoved. After all, it was not what the rich man did that sent him to prison, it was what he did not do that sent him to hell. By seeing need and doing the best you can to help meet it you are demonstrating the kingdom of God. But the rich man saw the need and did nothing. Did Jesus condemn any other more severely?

The brothers probably thought they were safe because they were descended from Abraham, just as

THE DANGERS OF WEALTH AND GREED   59

many who have no personal relationship with Jesus
consider themselves 'Christians' today. They, and we,
need a sign, but even a miracle will not melt hard
hearts. Faith is the only miracle we have.

So this parable demonstrates just how important our
present actions are. Money hoarded for selfish pleasures will bring disaster, but shared with the needy will
bring eternal blessings. Riches tend to separate us from
others and therefore also from God. Perhaps it can best
be understood in this undergirding cry for mercy: 'Is it
not to share your bread with the hungry and bring the
homeless poor into your house?' (Isaiah 58:7). This is
not a parable to condemn. But like much of Jesus'
teaching on money and possessions it is both a challenge and a warning. Jesus is, in effect, saying, 'I love
you. I have perfect plans for you. Please show my love
and your love united together by meeting needs you
come across. Just think of how long we are going to be
enjoying each other's company in heaven!' What a
motivation to put others' needs before our wants!

The parable of the soils
Matthew 13

*The seed cast in the weeds is the person who hears the
kingdom news but weeds of worry and illusions about
getting more and wanting everything under the sun stran-
gle what was heard and nothing comes of it.*

This parable describes a sower who literally sows
with wild abandon and hopes that some of his seed
will flourish. 'And the seed fell among thorns' would
probably mean land that also had seeds of weed in it.
The earth here had the potential to lead to a good

harvest but the hearer, although someone of intellect and passion, is not wholehearted. And this comes back to the division between irreconcilable loyalties: you cannot serve both God and money.

Worries about the world and the deceitfulness of riches literally choke the word. Worry destroys one's effectiveness and money can set itself up as an alternative master with its shallow promise of easy living. It is, in fact, possible to be so wrapped up in living our daily lives that we don't stop to think exactly how we are living. Are weeds strangling our relationship with Jesus? There is an old Russian fable that tells of a rich lady going to the theatre on a winter's night and weeping uncontrollably at fictional sufferings while her coachman was perishing of real cold just outside the door!

We all need to remember that not all seed that is sown prospers. Given the state of some of our 'soil' the rate of failure is not really surprising. These failures can be caused by a variety of things, including:

- our own spiritual short-sightedness allowing the enemy in to 'snatch the seed'
- opposition—Jesus never promised us a smooth journey, just a safe arrival
- worldly anxieties and the false promises of riches.

In this parable all the soils are said to have heard the word, but some are fruitful, others less so and some not at all. Are we letting anything get in the way?

The parable about seeking honour
Luke 14:7–11

The next time you put on a dinner party don't just invite your friends and family and rich neighbours, the kind of people who will return the favour. Invite some people who never get invited out, the misfits from the wrong side of the tracks. You'll be–and experience–a blessing. They won't be able to return the favour but the favour will be returned–oh how it will be returned! At the resurrection of God's people.

The story tells of a wedding reception where the host has to carefully appraise the 'importance' of the guests. Having money or power should not qualify people for the top places. They should go to those in closest relationship, regardless of wealth. None of us should strive for the top. Humility does not mean cowardice, low self-esteem or lack of enthusiasm. Rather, it conveys a sense of indebtedness. Everything I have has been provided for me by God and often by the work of others. The cult of the self-made person is a myth.

The parable of the persistent widow
Luke 18:1–8

A widow came and pleaded with a judge because she had been ill treated. The fate of people like her was often awful. They were often even cheated out of what little they had. Jesus' anger against the scribes and Pharisees who made a great show of lengthy prayer and yet at the same time took all that the widow possessed is clear (Mark 12:40). At one level this parable teaches us the need for persistent prayer. But at the surface level it talks of a judge who was obviously corrupt. He could only be dealt with in three ways: bribed, bullied or 'nagged at' until he gave in. The last was the only recourse to the poor widow. The judge feared neither God nor his fellow beings. But the widow would not stop.

She did not want revenge or punishment for her opponent in law, simply that she would be paid what was due to her. For a long time the judge ignored these pleas, even though he was supposed to give precedence to a widow's claim. He could, perhaps, just not be bothered but he is more likely to have been bribed and did not want to have to give it back. Eventually the judge decided he must hear her plea, probably because she was making such a fuss that he feared it would expose his corruption. Today there can still be injustice for the poor before the law. But where there is corruption or dirty dealing, God promises to expose it.

How 'religion' can corrupt true faith
Matthew 21:12-13

My house was designated a house of prayer but you have made it a hangout for thieves. Stop turning my Father's house into a shopping mall.

Jesus was furious when he came to the Temple, and described it as a den of robbers. His execution was actually instigated because of the insistence of the Temple authorities. The Temple was meant to be the ceremonial and spiritual centre of the Jewish faith, but it had become a political and trading centre as well. It was supposed to be a place of security and peace, but it had become corrupt and a place of quick profit-taking. It was no longer a place of prayer, but more somewhere a person would go to and receive automatic and immediate forgiveness of sins through paying for sacrifices. It was to this Temple that the blood money for Jesus' betrayal was returned by Judas and it was here, on Jesus' death, that the veil of the sanctuary was split from top to bottom.

When Jesus visited the Temple at Passover time it would have been especially busy, because visitors would have been coming from all over to visit Jerusalem at the time of this special festival. This would, of course, be just the time when traders inflated their prices because demand would be greatest–in exactly the same way as holiday prices are so much higher in school holidays!

At this time two kinds of trading would be taking place. First, there would be money-changing. Every Jew had to pay a Temple tax of half a shekel which was due at Passover time. After an initial period the tax could only be paid in the Temple itself and it would certainly have been there that almost all the Jews who were on pilgrimage would pay it. It had to be paid in high quality currency and so the function of the money-changers would be to exchange unsuitable coinage for the correct variety. To do this simple task, which took seconds, the money-changers' commission was about thirty per cent of a day's wage. What is even worse is that if the traveller did not have the correct amount to give and had to hand in a larger coin they would deduct a similar percentage from the change that was due. Usury was being practised in the very heart of the Temple, and Jew was robbing fellow-Jew at a rate that today's loan sharks would grab at. These charges were necessary to a degree to help pay for the upkeep of the Temple, but it was the extent of the corruption that so angered Jesus. Pilgrims who had come to worship would end up being exploited and the Temple money-changers made large personal profits out of them.

The selling of sacrifices was even worse. For nearly

every visit to the Temple some form of sacrifice was requested. If a leper came to have his cure certified or a woman came for cleansing after childbirth they would have to buy a dove for sacrifice. Such animals could be purchased easily from a variety of places, but all animals that were to be sacrificed had to be 'spotless'. At the Temple there were official inspectors of these animals who would almost certainly reject them and direct the poor pilgrim to the Temple stall-holders with whom they would have 'mutual understanding' or a 'working agreement'. Fraud is the more honest word that springs to mind. Even this got worse because a pair of doves which might cost half a shekel outside the Temple would cost ten shekels inside (but then of course they were guaranteed whiter than white). Not only that, but most traders were actually priests who were actively exploiting the very people who had come to find God through them!

And what do we sell at our temples today? At one cathedral shop I could buy candles, crucifixes, T-shirts and imps (bit of a give-away that), but they didn't sell any Christian magazines at all. We actually steer people away from our God in the name of religion or profit. No wonder Jesus got angry. Jesus could not bear to see people exploited but when he saw it being done in his Father's name, no wonder he exploded. But how do we react? Too often, sadly, I am silent in such a situation. Surely the Church needs to protect the vulnerable and the gullible?

Jesus' anger was aimed at those who put things in the way and prevent ordinary people worshipping God. In all the tension of buying and exchanging, prayer became impossible. And the people who sought God's voice found it was drowned out by

God's so-called servants. Power, tradition and prestige can today also create an atmosphere where prayer is impossible. Unlike most anger, Jesus' was not negative. He was angry because he so desperately loved those who were drawing near to his and their Father and he so wanted them to be able to have peaceful communication with him.

Paying taxes
Matthew 17:24–27; Matthew 22:15–21

It is quite clear that Jesus tells us we should pay what is outstanding, whether it be debts or taxes. In the first passage he is in effect telling Peter: 'You're a skilled fisherman. Go back and do a day's work. As you catch the fish you'll be building up a catch which you'll be able to sell and which will enable you to pay your taxes.' In the same way a secretary pays for her new coat as she types her bosses' letters, or the pilot pays for her holidays as she flies others abroad on theirs. God our Father has given us all a variety of gifts and we should use them for the good of both ourselves and society.

In Jesus' time there was much unrest about the Roman occupation and particularly the imposition of a poll tax. While there was no real argument about the need to pay taxes, the problem was that it was paid to a foreign ruler, Caesar, and appeared excessive. As such, it was hated by the Jews and the introduction of it caused widespread rioting (you would have thought Maggie Thatcher might have learnt this lesson!). Because of this the Pharisees were convinced they could trap Jesus because if he gave an affirmative answer to this question (which in fact he did), he could well lose the support and sympathy of Jewish patriots. On the other hand, if he replied negatively, for which they were secretly hoping, then he would have greatly upset the Roman authorities and even charges of treason could probably have been laid on him. Because the tax was so hated, Jews would only need the slightest hint that it was not the will of God to have a reasonable 'excuse' not to pay it.

At the end of the day the question is whether God's people are freed from the need to pay government taxes. The coin symbolises the authority of government and had Caesar's head on it, just as we have the monarch's head on our coins today. However, Caesar was regarded by many, including himself, as a god and this would be considered blasphemous by any good Jew.

In the complex financial situation at that time there were many different coinages. But this coin had to be used to pay the Roman taxes, just as the Jewish Temple tax had to be paid by the half shekel. Even though a coin belongs to the person who owns it, there is still a sense in which it says something about one's acceptance of the claims of the person who is depicted on the coin, and this is the point of issue here. If Caesar's rule is demonstrated by the coin, can a Jew possibly have such a coin because he would not acknowledge Caeser as head of his country? But Jesus says that the law must be upheld and dues must be paid.

By stating this it obviously means that Jesus is saying that God must be given what belongs to him as well. Perhaps his audience's motivation was to keep as much money for themselves as possible, thus depriving both God and government of what was really theirs.

PART 3

DEBT AND UNCONDITIONAL FORGIVENESS

Are you carrying any hurt?
Do some people owe you?
Have people let you down?
'And to think he/she calls himself/herself a Christian!'

Forgiveness is incredibly hard, but we need to be both able to forgive and to forget if we are to make real progress in our Christian walk. We also need to know how to repent and make any necessary restitution.

When I get to heaven I am sure there will be people there that I am surprised to see, but the person I will be most surprised to see is myself. I am acutely aware of my own failings but equally aware of God's forgiveness. In the light of the forgiveness I have received, any hurts against me are but minor irritations that need resolving and removing as soon as possible. Jesus teaches that all our debts (and even if we only did, thought and said one sinful thing each day on average we would each have 75,000 sins when we died) have been cancelled. How can I condemn others in the light of that?

The parable of the unmerciful servant
Matthew 18:21–35

The king summoned the man and said, 'You evil servant! I forgave your entire debt when you begged me for mercy. Shouldn't you be compelled to be merciful to your fellow servant who asked for mercy?'

This parable and particularly the conclusion Jesus draws from it cannot be repeated often enough. Can I really grasp that Jesus' forgiveness of me is directly linked to the way I forgive others? Yet I pray in the Lord's Prayer, 'Forgive us our debts as we [in the same way] forgive our debtors.' Jesus repeats this message throughout his teaching. He means it to hit home hard.

This story starts with Peter trying to show Jesus that he had a forgiving heart in that he was prepared to forgive someone seven times, whereas Jewish law limited this to three times. Forgiveness is not about arithmetic, it is about love and compassion. So this parable demonstrates the need for a forgiving heart.

In the parable Jesus shows extremes deliberately to highlight the points he is about to make. The first servant had an enormous debt to pay. In fact it was so large it was impossible to pay back. But the servant did not see it like that. He made rash and empty promises that if only he was allowed to he would find a way of repaying (how many creditors have heard these sorts of stories over the years?). What, in reality, he should have said was, 'Master, I owe you something that I am never going to be able to repay.'

The king had originally requested payment of what was due to him, but his compassion soon took over.

The servant asked for time, but the king did not release him on condition that he raised the money by a certain time. The debt is written off completely–something the servant never dared ask for because he knew it was something he did not deserve. And what we owe to God demonstrates both our many shortcomings and this unconditional love. There is no resentment, no claims for restitution, it is not grudgingly given. Such forgiveness is never easy. It carries enormous cost.

Once pardoned we do not have to fear that God will remind us of our failings. Nor will he torment us with the things that we didn't deserve to have forgiven. We only close the door to forgiveness by our own unforgiving spirit. For forgiveness suggests we have some to give as well as some to receive. By bitterly nursing our own resentments we can do much self-inflicted damage.

In the parable the servant who had just been released from the impossible debt deals without mercy with someone who owes him a trifling amount. He even 'seized him by the throat'. The Roman and Greek practice was to grasp a debtor by the neck of his toga and pull him half-throttled to court. They talked about 'choking the life' out of a debtor. Even more interestingly he says, 'Pay up. Now!' It is a general statement–one should pay one's debts. Given what the servant has just been excused, it is grimly ironic to put it mildly!

The second servant's plea is identical to that of the first. There are in fact just two differences: the amount owed and the response. We can only share the anger of the king because, having been shown outright mercy, the first servant responds to another with total unforgiveness. Mercy received must be reflected in mercy shown. Any wrongs we suffer are minute compared to what God has already forgiven us for.

> Earthly power does then show like God's
> When mercy seasons justice. Therefore
> Though justice be your plea consider this–
> That in the course of justice none of us
> Should see salvation. We do pray for mercy
> And that a prayer does teach us all to render
> The deeds of mercy.

> Shakespeare, *The Merchant of Venice*

In this parable the first servant interpreted his forgiveness as something personal, for him alone, that made him some sort of favourite of the king. Perhaps this made him feel he was somebody special and could therefore insist on having his puny debt repaid. His lack of charity shows both selfishness and stupidity. But to a greater or lesser degree, we are all like this second servant. We demand standards from others which we are incapable of fulfilling ourselves. We are so critical of others and so justifying of ourselves; seeing the splinter in the other's eye but not the plank in our own. What is pigheadedness in others is standing up for my rights in me. Your coarseness is my candid frankness. Your meanness is my thrift. And whenever I fail I can give you at least ten good reasons why. If only we were as considerate of others as we were of ourselves we would have far fewer disagreements and we'd all be a lot happier.

The world says that revenge is sweet, but it won't last long–it soon turns acidic. It can cause physical, mental, emotional and spiritual pain in the unforgiving person. God stands at the door and knocks, but revenge broods and magnifies imagined hurts so much that his knocking is not heard. Revenge is not sweet; it is poisonous, and that is another reason why Jesus came to pour out his restoring blood in an angry world so we could learn the true meaning of forgiveness. Our forgiveness needs to be total. We must try to forget. To move on. The last thing I want is that my miserable accounts of hurts done to me are kept, lest they come to haunt me when I stand at the judgement seat. After all, my sin brought about the death of God's only Son.

So when we disobey God in this way we are not so much sinning against law as against love. We are not breaking his law, we are breaking his heart. If we break the law there are penalties we can pay to atone for it. But a broken heart? All we can do is to show that we really acknowledge what the love of God has done for us, especially what Jesus did for us at Calvary, and then forgive others unconditionally.

Are there people who have hurt you in thought, word or deed? Is there money owing or possessions 'borrowed' that you have been moaning to yourself about but which in reality you could quite well do without? Whatever you need to put right, do it today!

The parable of the two debtors
Luke 7:35–49

'Two men were in debt to a banker. One owed five hundred silver pieces, the other fifty. Neither of them could pay up and so the banker cancelled both debts. Which of the two would be more grateful?' Simon answered, 'I suppose the one who was forgiven the most.' . . . 'If the forgiveness is minimal, the gratitude is minimal.'

The first thing we see in this story is that when Jesus was asked for a meal by Simon the Pharisee he accepted the invitation unreservedly. Whereas the poor would live in very small houses with just one room, the wealthy would live in much larger ones which would open out onto a courtyard. In warmer weather meals would be taken outside. The table would be a low construction and people did not sit on chairs to eat. They would either kneel at the table with their feet out behind them or, more usually, they would recline on their left elbow with the right hand free to eat and again with the feet stretched out behind.

At that time rabbis would have had a high profile and a big following. Wherever they went they would be followed by crowds keen to pick up even fleeting words of wisdom. So even when they were dining, people would come and stand behind them to hear the things they were saying. So then it is not that surprising that this lady had been able to get near Jesus. She would be just one of many who had come to hear what he might say that day.

Now Simon was a Pharisee, which means 'separated one'. He, like all others, would be dedicated to living out his whole life keeping every regulation of the law and would tend to look down on all those who did not do likewise. It is probable that he invited others as well as Jesus for dinner, but why did he ask Jesus? The first and most charitable possibility is that he genuinely believed that he had something important to say. Alternatively, he might have asked him round to meet with Simon's fellow Pharisees, in order to examine everything he said, find fault with it and possibly even start framing some charges against him. But the most likely option is that he simply liked being seen with someone who was getting a lot of attention–almost as if it would rub off on him. Some things seem to go across all ages and all societies! Yet because of their differences, Simon did not seem able to bring himself to offer Jesus the normal politenesses. He almost gave the view that here was an odd person, a bit disgusting but mildly amusing, who perhaps should be prodded about a bit.

The woman, in some cases referred to as Mary, was a well-known character–but for all the wrong reasons. She was the village prostitute. She would likely be ignored by the women altogether and only spoken to by some of the men secretly when they wanted her favours. They all would, of course, deny knowing her. It would have been bad enough for Jesus to speak to a woman in public, but doing so to a prostitute and letting her wash his feet. Well, whatever was the world coming to?!

The latter was a very good question because it was changing as never before. Something about Jesus had melted the woman's heart. Maybe she had heard him speak about sinners and, unlike the others present, was publicly willing to admit she was one. She could go on as she was no more. Her barriers gave way as her tears fell on Jesus' feet. Letting down hair was regarded as indecent for a woman to do, but Mary was past caring. She had lost her self-consciousness, she no longer cared about what people might think. She wanted to wash and dry the feet of her Saviour. Mary, one gets the picture, had a generous nature but she had fallen so often she had almost become a slave to sin. She no doubt hated the bondage she was in, the isolation she felt, the abuse she suffered. But no Pharisee had tried to help her. They just added to her pain by condemning and avoiding her. But Jesus had reached out. Even before she touched him, his words had touched her. God's peace had shone in her tormented soul.

Mary's tears were probably a combination of her previous shame and the great mercy now being shown her. And then Mary took the most precious thing she possessed—a bottle of expensive perfume, and anointed Jesus' feet with it. The breaking open of this phial could be saying several things, including that anything of material value becomes of insignificance compared to the joy of knowing the presence of the Lord. It could also signify the breaking free of her sinful past.

For whatever reasons, Simon was watching amazed. He would probably not believe that Jesus knew who she was, or what she was. If Jesus was a proper prophet he would be able to see what kind of woman Mary was. But Jesus not only knew who Mary was, he also knew what Simon was thinking— and that is why he told the story of the two debtors. Jesus simply asked Simon the question 'Who do you think would be the most grateful. One forgiven a small debt or one who was released from a large one?' Simon answered what we would also all acknowledge, 'The one who was forgiven the most.' Mary loved Jesus so much because she knew how much pain and heartache she had been released from.

The analogy of the debtors is very real because anyone who has been in debt will know of the real fear and sense of hopelessness it brings. At Credit Action we recently received an anonymous letter in which the writer said that debt had been a problem for them for ages, but they had bought one of our books some time ago and worked stringently at escaping from it. The letter concluded: 'For the first time in seventeen years I am free from debt. I will now get on with the rest of my life.' Those who are released from great debts experience great freedom, just as those who receive great forgiveness show great love.

It is interesting to note, too, that Jesus is not categorising sins. He is not saying that Mary's sins were worse than those of others. It is the degree of recognition of one's own sinfulness that is all important. In fact, Jesus seemed to treat sins of emotional excess less sternly that he did the sins of pharisaic pride or deliberate selfishness. Perhaps because it is precisely those sorts of sins that prevent us from 'seeing' the real us. So Jesus will have pity on and forgive a prostitute but will criticise self-righteous religious leaders: 'You brood of vipers.' Mary's sin was not condoned but it was forgiven; and only Jesus can make people rise up above their broken pasts and present struggles. The more we're aware of our shortcomings the more we can honour Jesus for all he forgives us for.

> For none, O Lord, has perfect rest
> For none is wholly free from sin
> And those who want to serve you best
> Are conscious most of wrong within.

> Henry Twells, 'At even, 'ere the sun was set'

Simon was self-righteous. It was honour enough for Jesus to be invited to his house; he didn't have to do any more. So even though the roads of Palestine were very dusty and sandals gave little or no protection, Simon could not be bothered to provide his guest with the usual courtesy of a servant washing his feet with clean water. He didn't want to waste money by fulfilling the normal custom of perfuming his guest at the dinner table. Nothing was done for Jesus by his host, but forgiven Mary did not stop kissing his feet–a sign of deep respect. Mary washed his feet with her tears, dried them with her hair and anointed them with her perfume. She had performed all the acts of hospitality that should have been done by Simon.

It is only when we realise just how much Jesus has done for us that we can really begin to love him as we should. I need to know that it is my sins that crucified Jesus, yet he still loves and forgives me. Mary knew from just how much she had been saved. Her life had been so dark that when the light shone, it had a piercing brightness. But Simon was already blind to any darknesses in him. He didn't think he needed saving from anything. He had, after all, grown no weeds, but neither had he grown any flowers–he was too dry. Mary's nature brought forth fertile soil in which both weeds and flowers grew. Even before Jesus did the weeding her garden was not devoid of beauty, but when he'd finished he'd created a perfect place of rest. He forgave her sins and told her to 'go in peace'. The meaning here is that she would be moving into a life of peace, joy and contentment that she had not previously known.

Those reading this book who are not murderers or rapists need to be so aware of creating league tables of greater and lesser sins. The sorts of sins that attract high profiles (which would include crime and sexual unfaithfulness as well) are often seen as being the only serious ones. But there are other sins only seen by those who live with us. They cannot be punished by law, but they might cause a lifetime's unhappiness. Sins such as selfishness, criticism and moodiness can really damage our partners and our children, but the rest of the world is unaware. Sometimes the sins of passion can be understood because of the flood of compassion that is in the same person. In any event it is clear that it is only when we are fully conscious of our sinfulness that we recognise just how much Jesus loves us and has forgiven us.

As the parable of 'the unforgiving servant' reminds us, keep on focusing on forgiveness.

The story of the prodigal son
Luke 15:11–32

Undisciplined . . . he wasted everything he had . . . but when he was still a long way off his father saw him. His heart pounding, he ran out, embraced and kissed him . . . 'My son is here–given up for dead and now alive.'

I have always loved this parable. Perhaps it is because I so easily identify with the prodigal that the Father's welcome and forgiveness still overwhelm me. I find Keith Green's song, *The Prodigal Son Suite*, about this story especially moving. But it is in fact a story about two sons. In Jesus' audience were sinners and also the Pharisees (the self-confessing righteous). Everything in this parable reverses this position as Jesus relates how those who are found are brought home.

As we have seen, under Jewish law a father left two-thirds of his property to his eldest son and one-third to the younger. But the younger son in this story was far too impatient and wanted his share immediately. What he was actually saying was, 'Father, I wish you were dead so I can have now what will be due to me.' It is self-will. The home was dull to the young son. He didn't like the rules and regulations. His father restricted him through love and his brother was plain boring. There surely must be more excitement out there. The grass looked greener and he was going to find it. Life certainly was not going to pass him by. And so the rebellious young son demanded the privilege of his inheritance without accepting the responsibility.

The young son was probably in his mid-teens as he would be likely to marry at around eighteen years old. In his hurry he is prepared to cut himself off from his roots. He has no moral regard for any obligations he may owe his father. Indeed, he deprives himself of any further claims to his father's estate, as he later acknowledges. He wanted independence and his father granted him his wish. Normally, the elder brother would have acted as mediator in such a crisis, but no mention is made of this. Perhaps there had already been a rift either between father and elder son or the sons themselves. Perhaps it was because if the father granted the younger son his portion he was likely to grant the elder his as well, although still retaining the titular ownership.

In any event, the younger son's request was granted. The son quickly set about calling in loans and selling land and other assets for cash so he could go on his carefree way. In those days large numbers would leave their countryside homes and look for money-making opportunities in the big cities. But this son's motives were different. He wasted the money recklessly on instant pleasure seeking. He chose a distant country as he wanted to get as far away from the old 'restrictions' as he could. Thus he would be able to express himself, to be who he really was. But this wild living soon meant that he spent all his money. Incidentally, we are only told his spending was wasteful. His elder brother may have accused him of spending it on prostitutes, but there is no confirmation of that. But, however he squandered it, it all went pretty quickly, as did the 'friends' who thought him great company as long as he was splashing money about. Living like this wastes talent and damages both mind and body. It can lead to bondage and addiction. It certainly soon leads to destitution. The young man's spirit became as tattered as his designer-label clothes.

At the time the land would suffer a major famine approximately every twenty years, so the pressure of this would be well appreciated, particularly when knowing the Jewish saying, 'When a son in need in a strange land goes barefoot then he remembers the comfort of his Father's house.' But the son would not go back. To do so would mean living off his elder brother and facing the scorn and anger of those he had left behind. He saw no alternative but to find work where he was. And he was in such a desperate state that he ended up working for a Gentile, who probably took sadistic delight in getting a Jew to keep pigs. This kind of work was normally refused by Jews because pigs were considered unclean animals. Having to feed them was about as degrading a job as a Jew could get. Wanting to share their food showed the depths of his despair.

With no friends left, the young man had plenty of time in his loneliness to reflect on events and come to the sad but inevitable conclusion that it was entirely his fault that he was in the position he found himself in. Any man who lives and spends selfishly becomes a slave of selfish desires. Coveting the lusts of the

flesh leads to the body mastering the mind. Loving
money can lead to horses or the lottery becoming an
addiction. But there is still hope. We, too, like the
young man, can come to our senses. It is not just a
figure of speech to say, 'He is not himself today.' Jesus
does not underplay sin. He stresses both its signifi-
cance and its tragic consequences. But he would not
believe that sin was the inevitable act of hopeless
humanity. He believes we can, must and will repent.

In this case the younger son was prepared to say
sorry, to ask for a job, to face the rejection of others. In
doing this he was trusting that his father would sort
the rest out. He even offered to be a hired hand, the
lowest of all servants, who literally relied on the good
will of their master on a daily basis to keep their job.
He simply knew he did not deserve any better and so
was prepared to swallow all his pride. He had squandered money and possessions, upset his father, been
an appalling steward and totally ignored God. Even if
he had not actually been disowned, he knew he had
surrendered all right to be called son. He just knew
that servants in his house were well treated.

So he acted swiftly and decisively. He was prepared
to go to be the lowest of the low. But one of the most
significant things about the parable is that he never
ever gets to make such a request. And he is about to
receive the same reception that all sinners who turn
their back on God and do their own thing get when
they turn back to him in desperation. Motives, as with
the young son, can be mixed. Even the best can have
some hidden agendas. But God, in his mercy, accepts
all those who turn to him. We don't understand why,
but we're so grateful that he does. So, hunger may have
driven the young son home but it would be mixed

with memories of his father's love and shame for his treatment of him. No doubt the son went over and over what he would say on his long return journey. His confession was real, with no excuses. He pleaded no extenuating circumstances. But he never got to be heard by his father. The speech of regret, rehearsed as he trudged painfully along the same road on which he had set out so expectantly, was never completed.

For the father was searching the horizon for him. He missed him, like he misses each one of us when we go off on journeys of our own without him. He ran to him. A man in Palestine of the father's age would never run, it was too undignified. But his love was so strong that humiliation counted as nothing. So, in a sense, he took on the shame that was due to the young son. He embraced and repeatedly kissed him. This is not just a sign of forgiveness, but a restoration of relationship. And it is the father who takes the initiative. The young son may try and spit out his apology, but his father is not listening; he is simply too excited that his lost son is back home.

The instructions that he issues show the extent of the welcome to be given. He is dressed in the robes appropriate to that of a son, not a servant. He must have a good clean robe because of his status. And he must wear the family ring as a symbol of his authority. He must also wear sandals to indicate that he was a free man and not a slave. Sandals would be worn in the house by members of the family only. Even guests would remove theirs on arrival. So, not only did he receive freedom but authority and possessions as well. He had been saved and set free and restored to his sonship while still being hopelessly lost. Just as Jesus received sinners and ate with them (Luke 15:2)

without receiving any signs of repentance, so the
father accepts his son before he has proved himself
truly sorry. And it is in simply acknowledging 'I am
not worthy' that the Father's unconditional love can
truly flow. By doing so one can be fully restored to
our heavenly family.

We must remember that however far we have been
away; however we have wasted money and/or possessions, our Father is scouring the horizon for us. He
instantaneously recognises us, even in our rags. He
knows our walk, every feature memorised, thought
about and wept over many times as we have ignored
his entreaties. And when we return there is no sharp
word of warning, no deep questioning to ensure
proper guilt, no probationary or quarantine period
until convinced that our weaknesses have been cured.
Just the unconditional fullness of our Father's perfect
love. We receive total forgiveness–and there is no
forgiveness that does not restore.

And so the fatted calf is sent for. A special animal
for a very special occasion. On his departure the
younger son had vowed never to return. To all intents
and purposes he was dead. His longed-for return
thus led to great rejoicing and this was meant to be
for the whole community.

While this was happening the elder brother was out
working. He was not summoned and one can only
conclude he was not on good terms with either father
or brother. Was he fed up with his father worrying
about his younger son or was he simply a workaholic
slaving away at what was 'really important'? At any
rate, when he does find out his reaction is to make us
rethink what 'sin' really means. Like the Pharisees he
remained apart from the 'sinners'. Jesus said the

greatest gift is love. The Pharisees would have seen
the younger son's sins as the bad ones. How could
they be forgiven so easily? Even today we will drive
people out of society for such actions while splashing
their weaknesses across the tabloids. Sins of passion
are all we seem to concern ourselves with. Jealousy,
pride, anger, judgementalism and unforgiveness don't
even seem to be counted as sins. They are rather
faults of character. But Jesus told the Pharisees that
prostitutes would enter the kingdom before they did
(Matthew 21:31). He treated sins of passion with pity,
but treated sins of self-righteousness with sharp condemnation. The woman caught in adultery was forgiven, as was the 'sinful' woman who anointed Jesus'
feet: 'Your faith has saved you. Go in peace' (Luke
7:50). But the Pharisees were regarded as hypocrites
and called 'snakes, broods of vipers and empty
tombs' (Matthew 23). So the prodigal receives a kiss
and the Pharisees receive anger.

The elder brother represented the Pharisee only too
clearly. He resented the fuss over the younger brother
who was so 'bad'. He had behaved impeccably.
Further, now he was back would he lose some of his
inheritance? In any event he refused to fulfil his role
as elder brother and go to the feast. Instead, he pre-
ferred to humiliate his father in public than risk losing
face. By quarrelling in public he demonstrates a break
in the relationship just as with the younger son years
earlier (see Esther 1:12). He was equally rebellious.

I have to say that if I was going on a week's holiday
I would probably not choose the elder brother to
come with me! The prodigal may be unstable and
morally suspect, but he would be generous, enthu-
siastic and a good companion. The elder brother,

always eminently respectable, would be tight, legalistic and petty minded. We are not called to be like the prodigal, but Jesus wants us to steer well clear of jealousy and arrogance. In fact, if I'd had an elder brother like the prodigal I too might have left home as soon as possible! He could have responded by thinking about how glad his father must feel or what a relief it must have been for his brother to return home safely. But he was too angry, too critical of both father and brother. Surely he was prodigal too? Yes he was dependable, hard working and loyal. But he was ungrateful. Most of his good fortune was a gift. He had sat daily at a well-stocked table. And so it is today with the respectable, who would never do anything that would cause any scandal but who never thank God for mercies shown; rather, they condemn those who have fallen so low.

The elder brother was also self-righteous. He was convinced he had been badly treated. If you believe in your own goodness it is hard to improve. He also lacked love, perhaps the 'biggest' sin. Home is where we should be real, where we can pour out our dreams and plan together. But the elder brother was not really there, he was not part of the family as such. He was too wrapped up in his own self, too critical of others and too aware of his own imagined hardships to even begin to understand his father's joy at seeing his son again. Life without love is surely wasted.

The elder son denies his brotherhood by referring to the younger son as 'this son of yours'. His father makes an attempt at reconciliation. He pleads with the elder son to enter, humiliating himself again in doing so. But this time the reaction is of complaint and bitterness. His good point, the elder son says, is obedience, but he has lost relationship and is looking for reward. Having clung to his inheritance he is exhibiting an opposite but equal selfishness to his carefree younger brother. But he sees himself as vastly superior. Surely this cannot be what it means to be a Christian! Pride, judgement, superiority must lead people away from Jesus. That is why the father pleading with the elder son is equally important. He, too, must simply accept his father's love.

When people live in unity they hold on to things lightly and share as is needed. It is not about what is mine and what is yours. We all need each other. Often the downtrodden, poor, unemployed, very young or very old, are ignored by the better-off who are too wrapped up, like the elder brother, in themselves. In this parable the young man's dignity was restored, but the money and possessions he squandered were not returned. He had to lose all material things before he would find his true inheritance through unconditional love. We too can live our lives enclosed in a comfort zone that money and possessions give us. A father who leaves too big an inheritance to his children may make it harder for them to find God. So it is ironic that those who accumulate riches to help their children will in reality often be doing the opposite. The elder son became self-centred and judgemental. At the end of the parable his father has offered him unconditional love and invited him in to the never-ending feast. No one has shut him out. But he would not go in because of his lack of love and because other things mattered to him more.

But by simply saying, 'I am not worthy', we can all experience the Father's love today!

Using money for repentance–Zacchaeus the tax collector
Luke 19:1–10

Jesus wants to meet with everybody. Anyone who turns to him will meet with him. Jesus will let no obstacle get in the way. When Zacchaeus spoke to Jesus and was accepted he responded not only with joy but also by promising to use his wealth, whether honestly or dishonestly earned, to feed the poor. Wherever he had done wrong he would also gladly make restitution and pay generous compensation as well.

In the past Zacchaeus had obviously been none too scrupulous in the way he extorted taxes. He probably had a very guilty conscience. But meeting with Jesus was not just a sign of fellowship, it was a means of receiving forgiveness. Zacchaeus also spoke openly to the crowd. He did this partly so that Jesus would not be so strongly attacked for dining with a 'sinner', but also he wanted to make a public statement about the changes that were going to take place in his life from then on. He was making himself accountable. To demonstrate his change of life he went beyond a mere statement and did something about it. So it is both a putting right of past wrongs, as in the case of giving to those from whom he had demanded too much tax, and also an expression of grateful thanks to Jesus, by feeding the poor.

In this way the true meaning of Christian discipleship when it comes to money and possessions is clearly demonstrated.

PART 4

USING MONEY AND POSSESSIONS IN THE SERVICE OF CHRIST

Servanthood seems out of place in our society with its emphasis on the rights and freedom of the individual. Sadly this attitude has often spilled over into the Church in that it frequently appears that what God can do for me is far more important than what I can do for him or for others. But we are called to serve—unconditionally and sacrificially. We are not to count the cost. We are to give generously and put others, made in the image of Christ, before possessions. In so doing, Jesus tells us that we are actually serving him.

The parable of the workers paid equally
Matthew 20:1–16

Friend, I haven't been unfair. We agreed on the wage didn't we? So take it and go. I decided to give to the one who came last the same as you. Can't I do what I want with my own money? Are you going to get stingy because I am generous?

This is often seen as quite a puzzling parable and for some time I felt it was unfair. This probably only goes to show how much the values of our culture and society invade us without our consciously recognising it.

In Jesus' time, hired servants would always be employed by the day and would receive their wages on the same day. 'Do not take advantage of a hired man who is poor and needy, whether he is a brother Israelite or an alien living in one of your towns. Pay him his wages each day before sunset because he is poor and counting on it. Otherwise he may cry to the Lord against you and you will be guilty of sin' (Deuteronomy 24:15). So the workers lived on the edge of destitution, having a hand-to-mouth existence and really needing work every day.

There were certain times of the year when this story could have been relevant in Palestine. For example, it would be particularly relevant at the time of the grape harvest (August/September). By the middle of September the rains would come and therefore it was always a race against the clock to get the crop in on time. So workers were urgently needed. The Jewish working day started at 6 am and finished as dusk approached at 6 pm. And so the parable starts with the owner going to the market place (the equivalent of the Job Centre) at the crack of dawn to hire workers. He is in need of workers and since there is a full day's work ahead they can negotiate their own terms. Three hours later, realising his need for more workers, the owner comes back and hires some more men. They are obviously in a less favourable position than the men already hired, but they agreed to work when they were promised a fair wage. This happened again at noon and at 3 pm. At 5 pm we again see the owner returning to the market place where he hired the remaining workers. By this time the shadows would already be lengthening and little actual work would be possible.

What motivated the owner to behave in this way? Practically, he might have sensed a change of wind, noticed the clouds beginning to build up and thought that this was his last chance to get his harvest in. Or, as the day wore on, he might have thought more and more about those left behind, those who were feeling increasingly hopeless, and decided to bring them in so they would not starve. Before he hires them the owner checks to ensure they genuinely want work by asking them why they are standing around doing nothing. If they had been idlers they would have come up with all sorts of excuses–perhaps the heat, their personal ailments or the government of the day–but they replied truthfully, 'Because no one hired us.' These men would have been there with their tools since dawn and would be feeling increasingly desperate about how they were going to feed their families. The fact they were still there at 5 pm proved just how much some pay, any pay, was needed. These were hired labourers, the lowest class of workers, and life for them would be hard at the best of times. Servants and even slaves would be attached to a family and at least therefore receive regular food. But being unattached the hired workers were totally dependent on chance employment. Just being out of work for one day would mean that the children would go hungry.

At the end of the day the workers get their wages and those who started late got paid first. They were delighted to receive what they had heard the earliest workers negotiate at dawn. And the other workers were delighted too–if those who had only worked one hour were being paid that amount, how much more would they receive? Imagine the outrage when everyone else got no more–'It's just not fair.' The owner talked to the workers and explained that he was being fair to them but he was also being generous to those who had not been originally chosen. It is so easy for us, too, to think of things from a self-centred perspective and therefore we condemn others or are jealous of their good fortune or lack sympathy for those who are hurting.

One thing is very clear. The hero of the parable, the vineyard owner, would get short shrift from his auditors! He doesn't calculate accurately how many men he needs for the day and then significantly 'overpays' many of the hired men. Further, he seems more concerned with their needs than their productivity. This would not have been the day to do a time and motion study!

So, this parable confronts those who merely see God as a god of justice, because hope, mercy and compassion is evident here as well. It also upsets those who regard themselves as especially pious and therefore deserving of special favour. Jesus accepted and mixed with sinners, even those who had shown no sign of repentance (Matthew 9:10–11), and the inclusion of tax collectors and prostitutes in heaven on an equal footing (would it be the homeless and addicts today?) is often too much for the 'religious' to accept.

This is an amazing parable because so many principles can be drawn from it. These include:

● *Jesus is concerned about every aspect of our lives, including our work.* If someone refuses to work then this would not apply, but if someone is desperate to provide for family and cannot because of the selfishness of others or the scourge of unemployment,

Jesus is deeply affected. For most of his life Jesus, as the village carpenter, was a working man. He would know how hard it was to support a mother together with his younger brothers and sisters. He might even have delayed starting his ministry until others were able to take over the roles of being family providers. In a true Christian society no one's skill should be left to rot. If only the labourers hired first thing in the morning had offered a fraction of their wage to those left behind, God would have honoured their sacrifice.

● *The quality of the work.* Although there is no suggestion that those who were engaged last worked better than the others, it would be true to say that a small amount of work done carefully is more useful than a greater amount done either more lackadaisically or easily. For example, if you knew you could win a prize for a crossword and there was one clue you could not get then you would really appreciate the person who told you that last correct answer!

● *The need for a living wage.* The estate manager could easily have cut the wages of the late-comers, but he knew that if he did so people would go hungry. Jesus is concerned about feeding our bodies as well as our souls.

As well as these practical issues there are spiritual issues too. For example:

● *Jesus v. Gentiles.* It is possible that this parable is a warning to the Jews. They saw themselves as the chosen people, as those who had special privileges. They tended to see God as a judge and therefore he would give to people precisely what they had earned.

But God is our perfect Father and he does not give more love to one son than to another.

• *Long-standing Christians*. Similarly, it is a warning to those who come to Jesus early in life or have always been Christians. They do not automatically have the right to dictate Church policy. God is always on the move and yet new blood or the rise of an ever more radical generation with different ideas and methodology can often seem threatening and needing to be put down at all costs. In fact those in this position have received a real honour and probably avoided much heartache as well. They must therefore not look down on those who come to Christ later in life or judge them accordingly. All, no matter when they come, are equally special to God.

• *Heaven*. This parable also demonstrates that no one will have seniority in heaven. Our sacrifices over the years give us no advantage over others and this upsets those who believe in a 'return' and are looking for salvation because of good works. The only reward possible is to hear the words, 'Well done, good and faithful servant.' We are all dear to God. Whether we come to Christ at eight or eighty-eight he loves us equally. Similarly, the Christian who dies young will receive the same welcome in heaven as one who lives to a ripe old age.

• *The compassion of God*. Unemployment is a tragedy. Someone feels they are worthless, not valued and unneeded. Many of us, myself included, will know the shame and fear that redundancy brings. There are no more jobs for life. But God clearly shows that he cares about our needs and demonstrates that in such circumstances we should be like the estate manager

and give practical, compassionate help to those who
need it.

● *The generosity of God.* The manager's defence to
those who complained makes it clear that no one
received less than that to which they were entitled.
The only person who 'lost out' financially was the
manager himself. And he had the right to choose to
be generous if he wanted to be so. Their complaining
shows their selfishness and meanness of spirit and
sadly can often reflect our own irritation when God
seems to bless others when they don't deserve it half
as much as we do! God's love is not reflected in our
hours 'worked' for him. It is the love in which it is
done that matters. A successful businessman may
give £1,000 to a project when he could have given
much more. A small child may bring £1 which was
saved up for over a period of time. And it is that gift,
which has little material value, that inspires us so
much more. As long as we give ourselves sacrificially,
God will give generously to us.

● *The grace of God.* At the end of the day none of us
can earn what God gives us. We simply don't deserve
it. What God gives is just that, not 'pay' but a gift, not
a reward but grace. We should be very grateful that
God does not judge us with what we 'deserve', nor
does he pay us by time or piece work. It is simply
grace.

But the real lesson of the parable is that it is the spirit
in which work is done that really matters. The people
selected first agreed to a certain figure. They had a
'contract'. They agreed to work on condition they
were paid. As their later conduct demonstrated, all
that mattered to them was to get as much as possible

for their work. But with the others there was no contract. All they wanted was a job to do. They willingly
left the reward to the manager. And so it is with divine
judgement. If a worker bargains for pay he should
receive it, but that will have been the reward. But if
another accepts God's promises he will be justified.
God does not keep an account book noting whether
we observe certain religious regulations. It is what
motivates us and the actions that stem from that motivation that matters. Going to Church to feel 'good' or
earn 'brownie–points' only shows our own emptiness.
Look at my prayers! Look at my good works! The
Pharisee can exist in every age and in every one of us.

There are two real motives for work. One is to serve
our fellow men and women. The other is to serve
God. People can serve God as doctors, but equally
they can do so as bus drivers, butchers or road swee-
pers. Any useful job is done for God. We should not
ultimately work for pay but to honour God, because if
we do so with the right motive we will receive a
reward which is beyond compare. Many people
who have received large rewards in this world will
have a lower place in heaven because earthly rewards
were their only thought. Many others who have sacrificed financial rewards on earth for the benefit of
others will be lifted up in heaven. It is a paradox of
Christian life that those who look for rewards on
earth will lose them, while those who ignore such
things will receive eternal blessing.

This is equally true of those who have limited opportunity. Rewards in heaven can be given for handicaps
overcome as well as for services rendered. Some people's birth or character will give them a strong start in
life. Others will feel the reverse. Who will hire them?

They desire to serve God, but they cannot do so as they would wish. But God sees their intention, he sees their heart. One man has never had a problem with pornography. Another stubbornly resists the enemy every day for five years until in a moment of weakness he succumbs. Only God knows which of the two of them is the more victorious in this matter. Those whose strength is solid often despise those 'hired at 5 pm'. 'How on earth have they managed to get in here?' they complain, forgetting that standing in the scorching heat of the midday sun is harder for the one waiting hopelessly in despair than the one who has already received an assurance of his future.

So let us be glad when others are called. Let us have sympathy for those still awaiting their calling and those who seem completely lost. And let us share our blessings–our money, possessions and our gift of eternal life–with all those in desperate need.

The parable of the talents
Matthew 25:14–30; Luke 19:11–27

Good work! You did your job well. From now on be my partner . . . It's criminal to live cautiously.

Although there are differences between the two, there are such close similarities that there is some debate as to whether these are two different versions of the same story or whether Jesus told the story in slightly different format on two occasions. In any event, similar conclusions can be drawn from both.

A talent represented a large amount of money–it was actually a 'weight' of money. The story talks of a master going away for some time and entrusting his servants to be responsible in his absence and leaving them with various talents to help them. The comparison with the death of Jesus and our awaiting his return, our responsibilities and the giving of the Holy Spirit, are quite remarkable. In Jesus' day it would in fact have been quite common for wealthy men to travel abroad for some time. They might go to Rome, for example, either to meet a new emperor or ensure they would continue in their position. During this time the man would obviously not want his land to lie idle and become weed-infested and unfruitful. So he gave his servants money in accordance with their ability and expected them to act responsibly and maximise the return from the initial gift given.

This would always be a difficult time for the servants left behind. Other powerful men might try and take over the land in the master's absence. The local population, too, might have been glad to see the back of him. If the servants tried to defend the property in such times they might lose their lives. But if they switched allegiances and the master returned the same thing could happen!

The servants received different amounts: five, two and one talents. The first two servants immediately began diligently working at maximising their return. One can imagine the servant with five talents following the market closely, reading about the likely outcome of the crop yields. On the information gained he invested his talents so shrewdly that he made one hundred per cent return. The second servant, who was given two talents, may not have had the same intellect as his colleague, but he was straightforward and honest. He can be imagined as working hard at his task. For example, if he was working on a vineyard he would diligently prune, water and harvest. So it was by his own labour that he made the two talents four.

The third servant, however, behaved differently. He simply hid his money in the ground. By doing this he was not showing he was lazy as it was the traditional way of defending one's money. So his explanation is not to be read as an apology. He had only done what others would have done. He didn't think he'd done anything wrong because he'd kept his talent very carefully. This man is not bad. There is no sign of apparent sin in his life. He was responsible to the degree that he did not squander the talent. He even regarded himself as a good judge of character because he was convinced his master would be angry if his talent was lost.

God loves everyone equally, but we are given different talents, different abilities. We can be born with unequal giftings, opportunities and possibilities. But God has taken this into account. He wants everyone to have the same chance to prove themselves and that is why he only gives us the number of talents that we can cope with. That is why in the parable the man with five talents is congratulated on producing five more, whereas the man with two receives the same amount of praise (indeed the identical words are used) for producing but two more. And so the man with the one talent will hear those same words of approval if he would produce but one talent more. Not more than he can cope with, not as much as some others are asked for, but just what God knows he is capable of if he works diligently at the task. It may be useful to think of a talent as a coin with two sides. On the one side is written 'gift' and on the other 'responsibility'. And to the same degree that someone receives gifts (be they money, possessions, power or ability) so are they accountable. So we probably should not be coveting our neighbour's talents; we might well not be able to cope with the responsibility that goes with them!

It seems clear that, in this parable, Jesus is emphasising the role of the third servant. He was probably referring at one level to the phonies who were determined to keep the status quo. But Jesus teaches that faith is all about change and growth. It is about going deeper, looking forward, not back, and being willing to be led by the promptings of the Holy Spirit. Our walk should be an adventure. A closed mind and a hankering after the 'good old days' will not lead to growth. The third servant was too cautious, he was not prepared to risk all. Are we prepared to risk all for Jesus? The third servant played safe. He simply buried his coin as protection from theft. In doing so he knew it was secure and could not be lost, so there was no danger of him having to make up any shortfall out of his own pocket. Equally, he wouldn't have to spend long hours making the talent grow or lie in bed at night worrying in case his investments turned sour. But his talent was still needed to grow. It is very easy to look around and see people with more talents and come to the view that our meagre talent is not needed, it is inconsequential. But in God's kingdom every talent is needed and given for a purpose. For that reason there are no large and small roles to play, because we all have equally important things to do. The failure of the one-talent man is as damaging as if the five-talent man failed. So the third servant belittled the talent he had been given. He thought it worth little.

Furthermore, he lacked the crucial spirit of adventure. Nothing is achievable without some degree of risk. It we take risks for God like the two servants we will be rewarded, but if we just try and protect what we have been given we will lose everything. Jesus is looking for something from us–love and obedience. Fear is the opposite of love. Fear asks, 'How am I going to get out of this unscathed?' Love asks, 'How can I best serve the Lord?' And we should be aiming to say at the end of our lives, 'Lord, I have done my best to serve you.' We may not be equal in talent, but we all can be equal in effort.

It is easy to blame others or circumstances. The third servant tried to justify his action, or perhaps I should say inaction, by even blaming his master. But the punishment came because he did not try. When we use a talent we will almost always be able to do more with it. If we do not use our skills and abilities we will soon lose them. But if we have proficiencies, be they at business, sport or music, the more we practise and develop our skills the greater the tasks we will be able to achieve and the more we can benefit others and the better we can serve our Lord.

Take a look at the talents God has given you. You have not been left empty handed. Do not think because you have little money or possessions that you can do nothing. Everyone has talent. God gives nobody an empty hand. The world is not full of multi-talented people and you. God is not so much looking for extraordinary people doing extraordinary things as he is looking for ordinary people doing ordinary things extraordinarily well! Our reward is to hear him say, 'Well done, good and faithful servant,' which again emphasises that this was said to

the two-talented man as well as his more gifted colleague. So the question is not 'how many talents have
I earned?' but rather 'how many have you earned
compared to the number originally given to you?'
The response is to do with the level of faith we possess. Seemingly small things done in Jesus' name,
such as giving a cup of water to a thirsty person,
are much more worthwhile than great things done
for selfish or dishonourable motives. The widow putting her mites into the treasury collection has blessed
humankind far more than the riches of Caesar.

Remember, a talent hidden is likely to rot. A talent
gainfully employed will multiply, so that more will be
added to it, whereas the one left stagnant will just
seize up. That is why the taking of the talent from the
one-talent man and giving it to one who now has ten
is not so much a punishment but more a statement of
natural law. The ten-talent man in comparison is not
told, 'Relax, you've done your job.' He is given
greater responsibility and opportunities. A trust-
worthy Christian never retires!

Both parables refer to the return of the master and
the fact that all servants had to give an account of
their actions to him. I do not know when Jesus will
return, but I do know it will be one day. In any
event, I will have to give an account to him for
my actions. How have I been as a steward of his
money, possessions and talents that he has given me?
I have to keep praying hard: 'Show me the talents you
have given me. Help me to develop them and let me
use them as best as I can in your service and for your
glory. Amen.'

The parable of the last judgement
Matthew 25:31–46

'Master, when did we ever see you hungry or thirsty or homeless or shivering or sick or in prison and didn't help?' He will answer them, 'I'm telling the solemn truth: whenever you failed to do one of these things to someone who was being overlooked or ignored, that was me—you failed to do it to me.'

This parable has become such a conscious part of our Christian faith that it has been called on repeatedly to justify social action. It has been called 'the noblest passage in the gospel', and even a Jewish scholar asked, 'How many deeds of charity and love, how many acts of sacrifice and devotion have been accomplished through the centuries by the remembrance of these words?'

We are used to hearing this teaching. But to a few hearing it for the first time it would be shattering and almost considered blasphemy. Jews would feel that if they had kept the regulations of the law and not broken any of the ten commandments they would be all right. However, they also believed that because they were Jews they were already God's chosen people who would therefore receive special treatment and to all intents and purposes would be completely exempt from judgement. Then Jesus told them that their judgement depended on their reaction to the real needs of others.

God looks at our motivation. We can serve God well, despite our many weaknesses, if we have genuine compassion for others. It is so easy to think we can do nothing because we haven't got tens of thousands of pounds to give to the poor, we cannot build hospitals or eliminate poverty. But the point of this parable is that the examples given by Jesus cost very little and can be done by anyone: simple kindnesses done for our brothers and sisters made in the image of Christ.

We will not be judged by nationality or colour. Nor will we be judged by social standing or earthly importance, the amount of money we make, the job we have or the fashions we have followed. It is to do with unconditional kindness–and this can only really be demonstrated by actions. It is being hospitable to the stranger, clothing the naked, feeding the hungry. Not bowing to the great, but reaching out to the hurting people. The people praised in this parable did not even realise what they were doing. Their goodness just shone forth–not for some reward but because they saw specific needs and were touched by them.

Many people will do good if they can see a return in it for themselves. Some, such as in the case of corporate sponsorship, hope that it will reflect well on themselves in either increased sales or raised good will. Others may hope that the good deeds they do will lead to greater things being given back to them. Still more may enjoy the attention that their actions bring, basking in the thanks received for all they are worth. All of these are in fact doing good for their own sakes, whereas Jesus says those who really do good do so unconsciously.

Many things surprise us about this passage, which is perhaps why it is so strongly remembered. It reverses our normal human thinking. Even those who had been helping compassionately are taken aback. They had been kind without motivation. They saw a fellow human being with a pressing need and gladly gave up money, possessions and time to help meet the need. So it is not surprising that they asked,

'Master, what are you talking about! When did we ever see you hungry and give you something to eat?' This passage helps us realise that when we give this kind of help we are in effect feeding and clothing Jesus and, even more frighteningly, that if we withhold these things we are leaving him hungry and naked. But, even more so, Jesus is asking us not to judge people as beggars or homeless. We are not even to see them primarily as people who need to be led to Christ as some form of evangelical fodder. Of course we want to see everyone come to know Christ as their Lord and Saviour. But Jesus sees the pain on our streets and in the world, he sees our obsessions with self, money, prestige, and he asks, 'Can't you see with my eyes? Feel their hurt? Increase your compassion?'

On the other hand, those who were condemned were even more amazed. How could they have been unjust? They had kept 'the law'. They were guilty of no crime. They were respectable. Of course, if they'd known that the beggar at their door whom they'd sent away with a flea in his ear was the Lord they would have shown him every courtesy. Of course they would, because they would have perceived that advantage would therefore come their way. Jesus tells us that if we put out the fire of brotherly love we put out the love of life itself. What's more, there can be a certain kind of snobbery when it comes to giving. Many would give to a well-known person in short-term need, either because he might be given recognition or at least compensated later. The occasional respectable charity would be fine, but not those scruffy homeless people in the high street. We must not be selective in our Christian giving–we must try and help all those that Gods puts across our path in genuine need. And we can only do this if we are being good stewards. Holding on to money and possessions lightly, being prepared to give to those who have more need than we do. This can put us in difficulty. We may, on occasions, be taken for a ride. And, whereas we need to be sensible if in doubt, it is right to err on the side of generosity. God does not give us gifts according to what we deserve. And an unconditional gift given in love can have a great impact, even if the recipient uses it for purposes other than those originally asked for.

When we love God and our neighbours (especially those most in need of love) we are really living–and we are walking very closely with Jesus too. Without love we will die. The time we spend on earth is but a blink of an eyelid compared to eternity. God is not going to ask us to recite the Gospel of Luke or investigate our theological beliefs. He will ask us, 'What did you do that helped make life easier for others?' This is not some important question for the high and mighty. It is for us all. And it is based on the way we react with the people we come into contact with on a daily basis. We should not be able to stop ourselves. It should be the natural instinctive reaction of a compassionate heart that knows that all one's resources are in fact God's and are to be used wherever we come across these circumstances. It is so easy to be selfish. So easy to trample on our fellow citizens, sometimes by deed, but often by neglect. If we who are rich and gain interest on our savings do not give generously–perhaps to those who would otherwise have to borrow from loan sharks at exorbitant rates, for example–then the poor will be getting poorer at our expense. The help we give blesses God our Father in the same way as a human father would be grateful if we were to help his child. In one sense we can do nothing for God because he has and is everything. But to give to a child of God is something else–and it blesses God, the receiver and the giver!

Can we let go of things for the benefit of others? I heard a story of a very poor family. The daughter was being teased at school because she had no shoes. A neighbour sacrificed what little she had and bought her a pair of shoes, but the only trouble was they were black when everyone else wore white. So she was still teased, but at least she could walk comfortably. The teasing had hurt her deeply. One night she sobbed herself to sleep thinking about it. Then she had a dream. She saw Jesus come into her classroom in a radiant white robe. All the class wanted to be beside him, but he walked over to her. As he got in front of her he winked and lifted his cloak up a few inches. He was wearing black shoes. He identified with her.

I know of a couple who had never been abroad and were saving up to go away for the first time, for their silver wedding. They could afford to save £2 a week. After several years they were just about ready to book this special holiday when they heard of a pressing need nearby. After prayer they immediately gave everything they had saved to meet this need. They never told anyone else they had done this–only that they had decided to do something else instead of going away. And that is all anyone would have known, were it not for the fact that we have a wonderful and loving God who honours such obedience. Several weeks later a close relative of the wife won a competition. The prize was a world cruise for two but she couldn't go on it. There are no prizes for guessing who went on it instead and what a silver wedding celebration they had!

Holding on to things lightly, sacrificial giving. Both alien to our society, but bringing enormous eternal rewards.

The parable of the good Samaritan
Luke 10:25–37

'Which of the three became a neighbour to the man attacked by robbers?' 'The one who treated him kindly,' the religious scholars responded. Jesus said, 'Go and do the same.'

This is probably the best known of all the parables. Obviously, this can be a handicap to those who know it well, as the bluntness and unexpectancy can be lost. But just prior to telling this story, Jesus is confronted by a religious scholar who was trying to trap him in the finer points of the Law. When Jesus accepted his reply 'to love God . . . and love your neighbour' he was questioned further: 'And just how would you define neighbour?' The man was looking for a loophole to trap Jesus. It is quite clear from Jesus' response that the scholar knew the right teaching, but Jesus proceeded to demonstrate that it is vital to act upon it. The Jewish scholars at that time also believed that loving your neighbour just applied to their fellow Jews. Jesus had a shock in store for them.

The story that Jesus told would have been acceptable to his audience as far as the setting goes. Ambushes frequently happened on the Jerusalem to Jericho road. The road descended steeply and had many sharp turns and blind spots–ideal for robbers. In the parable there are four key players. First, the man who was travelling on the road alone. The audience would have assumed that the man was Jewish.

As most people at that time would have travelled in convoys, he was probably being reckless going on his own. Then there was the priest. Many priests when not on duty stayed in Jericho. The Jews had all kinds of superstitions that had almost become laws through constant following. One was that anyone who touched a dead man would be unclean for seven days. This in effect would bar him from participating in any religious service. So the priest might well have been genuinely concerned for the wounded man, but he daren't investigate in case he was dead and his ability to be a priest at the Temple was impaired. His position was more important to him than his compassion. Afterwards came a Levite. He too avoided the injured man. This again can be 'explained'. Often robbers would use decoys and one of their number would pretend to be wounded. When the passing traveller stopped the rest of the band would jump out and catch him unawares. The risk to personal security and the possible loss of money and possessions was too great.

Lastly, there was the hero of the tale–the Samaritan. These people were hated by the Jews and they had been at loggerheads for nearly 500 years. Because of their marriages with outsiders, the 'pure' Jews believed they had lost their right to be called the 'chosen people'. But in this particular case there is some problem with considering the Samaritan in this light. He appears to be some type of travelling salesman and the innkeeper obviously knew him well enough to trust him. The most likely explanation is that the term 'Samaritan' was used in contempt by orthodox Jews for any law-breakers (Jesus is himself referred to sneeringly as one in John 8:48), so the picture is of the orthodox passing by and the despised sinner helping out of his compassion.

This story incenses us just as it has pricked the conscience of humankind down the generations. The behaviour of the priest and Levite seems unbelievable. But can I be so sure that I would not do the same? Am I too busy with other good works to get involved? Is it going to involve too much time, money, effort? Perhaps it would be better to campaign for lights on the Jerusalem-Jericho road, or increase deterrent sentences for robbers? Perhaps it would be better to leave the man lying there and rush off and warn others coming the same way. Far easier for my hands to hold a petition asking for change than getting them bloody meeting the immediate need. Of course the government should do something about it and so should the council. Me? I'm sorry, but it's just not my responsibility. And so we excuse our own inaction.

'And just how would you define neighbour?' The question is self-condemnation. The answer is anyone who needs help. True neighbourliness does not look at boundaries. It looks not for limits but for opportunities. It is so easy to pass by people who are hurting and think they are nothing to do with us. We tend only to act if someone really close to us is affected.

The way Jesus tells the story forces us to put ourselves in the place of the injured man. The representatives of your faith pass you by. But then suddenly someone you might previously have ignored or even looked down on stops to help. Your attitudes can quickly change. The Samaritan just couldn't go on. He had to help and in doing so demonstrated that you cannot define 'neighbour', you can only be one. Both the giving and receiving of help cross all cultural and class barriers. All that is left is for us to put true neighbourliness into effect and the Samaritan shows us how. He was the only man travelling the road who really saw the victim. The priest and Levite saw an injured body and the Samaritan saw someone in his own likeness. How often do we really see people? How often do we glimpse through our self-erected barriers at others with similar barriers and think, 'Well, they'll want to keep themselves to themselves,' or, 'I'd better not interfere'?

A good neighbour does things personally. And the Samaritan certainly did that. He gave first aid to the man who had been robbed, disinfected and bandaged his wounds, lifted him on a donkey, led him to an inn and paid for his future care and attention. This is genuine Christian love in action.

The Samaritan also was prepared to accept his responsibility towards the injured man. Given that there would have been no inn on the deserted road, the man must have been taken to Jericho where he might well have faced both searching and hostile questions. But he stuck to his task. He did not even rely on the innkeeper as having similar compassion, but made advance payment for the injured man and assured him that if there was any money still outstanding he would settle up on his return. He therefore took all the right steps to ensure full recovery. In giving help he gave of himself.

Of course, help has to be organised and charities do this to good effect. Individual indiscriminate and emotional giving can quickly become harmful. But the concept of neighbourliness is to do with the individual. Love can only really radiate when life touches life. And Jesus calls us that as we go down our road we act as good neighbours to all those we meet who have fallen at the roadside. There is a cost to this. The Samaritan's donkey would be tired, its saddle probably stained with blood. His journey was interrupted, he may well have had to go out of his way to the inn and certainly would have been travelling at a slower pace. His business would have been harmed as a result. He also gave his money. Profits were secondary to him when compared with human need.

At the beginning of this passage it is clear that the scholar is self-centred. It is about what he has to do. His thoughts would primarily be with himself rather than with anyone in need. But Jesus shatters this self-centredness. He tells us we cannot say in advance who our neighbour will be. But he also tells us that it involves direct action. Jesus calls us all to 'do the same', to treat people kindly and be generous in our help. Further, this is not something to do occasionally but should be lifetime contact.

Being a Christian should dramatically alter all previously held views, values and opinions. Like the scholar, we need to grasp this to fulfil God's will. It will often mean painful dismantling of cultural and legalistic thinking. Unconditional love is our model and God our only judge. Yes, we will face the scorn of others, our privacy will be invaded and there will be a cost to our wallets as well as to our emotions. We have been set free to show God's unconditional love on earth. To show that people matter more than possessions. That someone else's need is more important than my want. We do not have to live in a certain way or conform to selfish ways. We have been set free! We are to put ourselves in our neighbour's shoes. To think 'there but for the grace of God go I'. In doing so, our ego is set aside. We can no longer jump in with excuses, however well reasoned out, for not helping. Nor can we judge the neighbour as someone who has brought this all on himself–for we all do silly things.

We should also remember that religious rules played their part in this story. Passing by a half-dead man equates to passing God by, because he is on the side of the hurting, the oppressed. The road symbolises our everyday life and such indifference to the weak is a sign of ungodliness, however religious we may appear.

The parable of the good Samaritan is timeless. It shows that pity which remains just an emotion is a sin. It must provoke action. Yet, if we substitute nationalities and occupations for modern equivalents we will really see that little has changed. A church cloaked in tradition, ritual and ceremony or a modern one totally wrapped up in 'signs and wonders' may be quite dead if it is not pouring out practical help to those who need it. And we, as individuals, must be prepared to take action, even if personal risk is involved. We may not want to get involved because our motives may be misinterpreted or because there will be a significant financial cost to ourselves and even a lowering of our standard of living.

So the parable of the good Samaritan is not about somebody doing a good deed once, rather like a boy scout. It is about taking down our barriers and keeping them down so that we truly see others and their associated needs. It is about deeds not words, our willingness to help, not respectability. It involves risk, sacrifice and the sharing of money and possessions. Everyone who hears and reads this parable cannot avoid the implications with regard to personal wealth. Jesus commands us: 'Do it and you'll live.'

Whenever we see hunger, suffering or oppression we must surrender ourselves and demonstrate the love of God by helping put things right.

The parable of the unjust steward (or crooked manager)
Luke 16:1–13

I want you to be smart in the same way—but for what is right—using every adversity to stimulate you to create survival, to concentrate your attention on the bare essentials so you'll live, really live, and not complacently just get by on good behaviour . . . You can't serve both God and the bank.

I, like many others, have struggled with the meaning of this parable. Briefly it tells of a master whose steward has complete control of his possessions. This was fairly common, particularly if the master, though wealthy, could not read or write. He could, for example, have been a money-lender where loans were paid in kind rather than in cash. In any event he seemed to be charging his master's tenants exorbitant prices and news of this got back to the master. The steward realised he had no defence and his job was on the line, so he negotiated deals with the creditors in an effort to gain friends.

Some scholars have argued that the steward was stealing from the master, who on learning of this had no option but to sack him and no one else would employ him because of his dishonesty. They then argued that by involving the creditors in his dishonesty they have, in effect, become accomplices and are therefore unlikely to appear as witnesses against him. Why he may even have been able to blackmail them in the future. On learning of this the master congratulates him on moving so speedily to protect himself. However, I think another explanation is more likely. The steward concerned would have received two sources of income. One was a low basic salary from his master and the other was a fee or commission which the tenants paid to him. He was therefore responsible for collecting two amounts: his master's rent, which went directly to the master, and his fee. I believe it is in the amount of his fee that the dishonesty took place. The official collection of Jewish oral laws specifically mentions this additional fee paid to agents (Ben Sirech 35:15–19) who would also expect to receive a 'little something under the table'. In this particular case it would appear that the steward was trying to get a lot in an effort to 'get rich quick'.

These amounts would not have been recorded in the bills and so the master could know nothing about these 'extras'. So the master was not overcharging nor was he receiving less rent than he should have been. But what the steward was doing was devaluing the relationship between his master and the tenants. The master's reputation would suffer and other people would be less willing to become his tenants if they knew they had to pay lots of extra hidden commissions. (Anyone who has had to try and cash in a fairly recently bought endowment policy may now be extensively sympathising with these tenants!) So the master is informed that his reputation is at risk. Immediately he wants to put right the wrongs done to the tenants, so he asks for the account books of the steward to be forwarded so that losses can be repaid and his reputation restored. It is in response to what the steward did at this stage that the master congratulates him.

When the master challenged him the steward

remained silent and he probably realised that any reply would just incriminate him more. His silence implies guilt, however, and he knows that he cannot get himself out of this mess by making excuses. Given the circumstances he would have expected to have been put in prison, but the master (who, as often in Jesus' parables, represents God the Father), although expecting obedience was also merciful. And so, although the master and manager knew he had been dismissed, others did not and this gave him a small window of opportunity to act decisively and minimise the damage done. So he accepted lower payments for himself.

The process of dismissal would take time. The steward will have to get his accounts up to date. After that he will be jobless. He doesn't think he is qualified to do anything else. So he decides he must come clean and reissue his bills to the tenants without his added excess commission. So the master applauded the steward for returning to fair and lawful dealings as it meant that he too would be looked at in a fair light. As stewards we too are not the absolute owners of 'our' riches and should not be taking either from God or from others on false pretences. This steward may have been deceiving both for a long period of time, but a quick turning about and genuine repentance will still lead to praise.

The steward also came to realise that ultimately people matter more than money. That friendship can last a lifetime but that money can soon melt away. By asking the creditors 'how much do you owe my master' he is confirming what is owed. But he only asks them to pay a portion of it. The rest he will repay out of the previous high commissions he had charged. So in repenting not only was he saying sorry, he was actually putting right as best he could the previous wrongs he had done very much in the same way as Zacchaeus offered to do to those he had charged too much tax. Obviously, being given an unexpected and unasked-for rebate, the tenants were highly delighted and they probably sent word to the master thanking him for his kindness. Given that he had received the full amount from the steward, he would realise that the steward was endeavouring to put matters right and restore his damaged reputation. And so the master commended the steward for astuteness, not his earlier deceit. It is the fact that the steward looked forward and saw what really mattered that is approved.

So this parable is first a challenge to our zealousness. Today a man of the world may go to any lengths to acquire wealth. He may work long hours and take no holidays. What little time he has to himself he spends in planning how to make more. He resolutely overcomes any things that get in his way. Are we Christians just as zealous? How much time do we give to work, sport, hobbies and how much to being with God? Would a downpour prevent me from going to church but not to the football or the cinema? Where is our determination and our all-embracing enthusiasm? Jesus is in fact saying, 'Where is your treasure?' For where it is there our hearts will be also.

This parable also challenges us to face reality. The steward looked at his situation and faced up to it. He refused to live in cloud-cuckoo land. He did not expect some miraculous answer to all his problems to suddenly come whizzing his way. He saw his weaknesses but he also knew his strengths. We know that fame can easily lead to ridicule, that over-spending can lead to debt and shame, and that rest easily turns to boredom. Do we fully recognise and utilise the strengths Christ has set in us?

We are also clearly challenged to look at our attitudes towards money. The parable tells us that we should use the material possessions God has given us generously so that we can develop friendships so that when reverses occur these friends will come to our assistance. Some people have seen money as evil. They have lived a hermit-like lifestyle and refused to have anything to do with material things. This is obviously wrong as people who live like this rely on the charity of others to survive. So what would happen if everybody decided to do likewise? Jesus had been the village carpenter. He made a living.

Others, sadly far too many, become servants of money. This can be the person who recklessly gets into debt by overspending, the miser who must have more and more hoarded or the person who works dishonestly to acquire more. When we are buying our lottery tickets we need to pause and think that our search for having much much more can be too costly on all involved.

But for some money can be seen as a useful resource–something to benefit others. By using material things in the correct way we will neither worship nor hate them, but use them to bring peace and beauty into our lives and to those whom the Lord puts across our path.

The parable also challenges us about our future. The steward sees problems ahead and immediately resolves to do something about them. It is so easy to hide from problems and hope that they will go away, only to find that they loom larger. I think of many people who have been in debt for months if not years before they acknowledge that they have to do something about their problems. And, more importantly, what about our eternal future? Do we prepare for it in the same way and with as much effort as we plan our pensions or even future holidays? Money used with love and compassion will bring light, peace and hope where before there had been only hopelessness. Giving to those in need is a sign of both good discipleship and self-denial. It shows a caring heart.

Once the steward realised that in his selfish pursuit of wealth he had also damaged his master he set about making recompense. The best way of doing so is to demonstrate the change of heart by outward altered actions. Today in our world money has been set up almost as a rival to God. So Jesus' appeal for us to hold on to it lightly is not so we can be blessed by doing good works, commendable though that is, but so we do not worship a rival that prevents us from entering the kingdom of heaven.

'You cannot serve both God and money' is a saying Jesus was fond of. Even if we have very little we can serve God by being faithful. Serving money makes us selfish, so we can't honour God and be selfish at the same time. So the way we handle our possessions is a clear indication of our real commitment to Christ.

Jesus concludes the parable by adding some teaching. In it earthly and heavenly wealth are equated with small and great responsibilities. We will not be entrusted with heavenly wealth if we have not been faithful with what is 'ours' in this world. We have to be seen to be obedient in the small things and at the same time have our priorities focused on God. As Christians we already belong to eternity. We are going to possess the treasure of heaven. Surely because of this we wish to be as obedient to Jesus as he was to his Father. We cannot divide this servanthood between two places. The Pharisees who 'loved' both God and money would not have liked such teaching. It made them look shallow. But, unlike the unjust steward, they were not prepared to repent and change their ways. However, if we really want to know Jesus and love him with an all-consuming passion we will become rich with a genuine eternal wealth.

The parable of the yeast
Matthew 13:33–35

In Jesus' day all bread would be made at home and yeast would make all the difference to the dough rising up. In the same way, Jesus helps us rise up over our difficulties. With Jesus we are completely changed, just as the dough is changed by the yeast. So we see ourselves as if magnified and we can see clearly what we are like, warts and all. We see that we fall far far short of Jesus and yet, at the same time, his unconditional love poured out on each one of us makes us want to honour him. Jesus also causes a social revolution. The world tends to judge someone by the amount of money they have, their power and prestige ('Hello, how are you and what do you do?'), but Jesus values us by the service we have given to others and by how we are honouring him.

Equally, there is an economic revolution. Jesus tells us that the hungry will be satisfied but the rich sent away with nothing. In a truly Christian condition we would have so much compassion for one another that none would be able to cope with having too much if others had too little.

So this parable demonstrates that, just as yeast disturbs the dough, so our faith should have a significantly changing impact on ourselves, other individuals we come into contact with and indeed the world.

The parable of the unfaithful servant
Matthew 24:45–51

This parable simply demonstrates that we should not be passively waiting around for Jesus to return. When he does return he will not be asking us if we got the date right. The question will be, 'What have you been doing?' So the faithful disciple need have no fear about the timing of Jesus' return. If, however, one thinks it's some way off or 'surely I won't die for years', there develops an attitude of 'when the cat's away the mice will play'. This will only lead to one being inevitably found out and severely judged. We must not waste what God has given us–be it money, possessions or talent. We must be accountable.

The parable of the Pharisee and the tax collector
Luke 18:9–14

Like some other parables, this contrasts two characters. A Pharisee–a separated one–who went so far beyond the requirements of the Old Testament Law that he just knew he was superior to others, was the first. He would be a pillar of his local synagogue, and well respected in the local community. He would consider that he would be defiled by having contact with others who were not so meticulously religious. Needless to say, he became arrogant. When he prayed it was almost as if he was congratulating himself on his achievements. He tithed everything. He looked around and saw a despised tax collector. He was glad he was not like him.

The tax collector, on the other hand, was fully aware of his own sinfulness. Tax collectors operated very much as some debt collectors work today. A fee would be paid by the tax collectors, who were then free to get tax in from individuals. They would often press people to pay far more than they needed to and so often made excessive profits. There were so many different taxes that people could easily become confused. And tax collectors were Jewish people working for the Romans. They were deeply despised. Yet it was precisely because the tax collector was humbly aware of his own failings that, Jesus said, his prayers were able to be heard.

We live in a society today that thinks like the Pharisees, where size of house and bank balance and importance of position demonstrate our thinking and reflect on how we see others. At the end of the day God will not ask, as the Pharisees seem to think he will, 'What did you *not* do?' Rather he will ask, 'What *did* you do to help others?' It's a sobering thought.

Giving
Luke 21:3–4, Mark 12:43–44

The truth is that this poor widow gave more to the collection than all the others put together. All the others gave what they'll never miss, she gave extravagantly what she couldn't afford—she gave her all.

It is often thought that Jesus said little or nothing about giving and tithing and that in any event the latter was under the covenant of the Law, whereas with Jesus we are now under grace. This is not usually said by people who want to give more than ten per cent. Jesus made it very clear that he came to fulfil the Law. And in Matthew 23:23 we read quite clearly that although Jesus vehemently opposed the attitudes of the Pharisees when it came to tithing, he still said it was right that they did tithe: 'Woe to you, teachers of the Law and Pharisees, you hypocrites! You give a tenth of your spices–mint, dill and cumin. But you have neglected the more important matters of the Law–justice, mercy and faithfulness. You should have practised the latter *without neglecting the former.* At the same time he tells us that our giving should be done quietly and without ostentation (Matthew 6:1–4).

Then, of course, we have the story of the widow's mite (Luke 21:1–4). Jesus recounts this as a talk about true and false religion. True Christianity impacts a person's attitude to wealth and brings out the important point that in God's eyes it is not the amount that we give that matters but the amount that we actually keep and spend on ourselves.

Jesus may have been physically able to see what the widow gave, although he would have to surmise that it was all that she had. Given that widows lived off the generosity of others though (and the fact that he possessed divine revelation helps too!) this was highly likely. In the Temple itself there would have been a number of rooms where valuables could be kept, one of which was known as the 'Treasury'. Here there were thirteen trumpet-shaped collection boxes for different offerings. They would depend on the purpose of the gift at that particular time. Jesus would know not only who was giving what, but also that the poor widow gave proportionately more than all the others. The rich gave out of their abundant wealth and it had little or no impact on their lifestyle. But the widow probably sacrificed real needs and gave away the little she had for the love of her God.

So Jesus tells us that tithing is still right, but that it is what we keep and our attitudes that are all important. So how does that mean we should give today? I believe Jesus is telling us the following:

- That we are still called to give to God.
- That our attitudes and priorities will determine what we do give and how willingly we give it.
- That all of us who are working should still be tithing.
- That those of us on good salaries could give an awful lot more than ten per cent if we chose to do so.
- That the equivalent of widows today, which would also include the unemployed, single parents, etc., who receive benefits that enable them to exist on the bare essentials, will be making sacrifices by giving anything. They should not feel under condemnation for not being able to tithe but should do so if they possibly can. However, giving £1 may mean they have to sacrifice a meal. Many others would not know they had even lost it.

Before we criticise the level of others' giving, before we rush off to have jumble sales or apply to the lottery for funding, we had better examine our own hearts. It is important to remember, too, that God has given us obligations here on earth. One of which is to ensure that we honour our parents and another is to look after our children. In neither case are we to spoil them, but we are responsible that their basic needs are met. Jesus got very irate with the Pharisees: 'Moses said, "Honour your father and your mother" . . . but you weasel out of that by saying that it's perfectly acceptable to say to father or mother, "Gift! What I owed you I've given as a gift to God" thus relieving yourselves of obligation to father or mother' (Mark 7:10–13).

Many become Christians and come into the kingdom struggling with debt. However hard it may seem, they should endeavour to tithe, even if it means moving to a significantly simpler lifestyle. As Dr R.T. Kendall says in his book *The Gift of Giving*, he did not come out of debt until he started to give God his tenth, finding that the ninety per cent went further. If you have reached the point where you are having to negotiate with creditors or courts this will not usually be possible, as the tithe would not be recognised in such arrangements. If you are in this situation seek help, because as God sees you trying to get out of debt and get your finances in order and give him the first fruits he will honour you in return.

Relationships before money
Matthew 5:23–24; Matthew 5:38–42

Jesus constantly emphasises that relationships matter more than anything else. In these brief passages Jesus emphasises this by saying that, even if we are worshipping God, even if we have got to the point of giving God our offering when we realise a relationship is wrong we should stop there and then and put it right. This is true even if it is our brother who is upset with us! We must always make the first move, always ensure that relationships are fully restored. We may have to do things to put them right. We'll certainly have to say we're sorry and we'll certainly have to demonstrate that we love people more than things.

This is confirmed in the second part of this teaching. The law at that time specifically forbade a plaintiff from claiming the cloak of a debtor because it both covered his nakedness and kept him warm at night as well. So this word is given to all those who fear they might lose everything. Jesus is saying in effect that if someone sues you, especially if their motives are suspect, do not fight back using the same tactics. So if someone wants to take your cloak from you then let them have your shirt off your back as well.

To respond in such a way means that you literally stand naked before both God and your accuser. It is a picture of a poor and destitute man being hounded by a merciless creditor–who behaves very much in the same way as the debtor forgiven a great sum by his master in Matthew 18. The poor man has no connections, no 'strings' he can pull, no one who can put in a good word for him. He appears powerless, but by surrendering everything he remarkably regains the initiative (this, of course, is a reflection of what Jesus has done for us on the cross).

Suddenly it is the creditor who is being ridiculed. Imagine that you are in a small village. You see a man grab another and demand his coat. The debtor proceeds to take all his clothes off and give them to his creditor and stands naked before all who pass by. The creditor would thus appear as a cruel and heartless person and would no doubt soon urge (or be encouraged to urge) the poor man to get dressed. This story thus helps show how the poor retain their dignity while at the same time exposes the evil that the 'haves' can do to the 'have-nots'.

Jesus is in fact also emphasising that we, as his disciples, should give without restriction or qualification–even if there is some negative impact on our lifestyles. Giving can often be done to establish power over somebody–to keep them in your debt, to enable one to bask in one's own 'goodness' or even so that others may commend you. So the benefactor somehow becomes a patron to whom the recipient is beholden. But a genuine disciple of Christ is one who will give without expecting any return from the receiver.

At the time of this teaching there were rich men who wanted to buy land that, because it was part of ancestral inheritance, was not on the market. The only way this land could be acquired was if the peasant farmers defaulted on their loans. The rich developed a strategy of targeting a farm at a time and operating in a way that made it inevitable that the farmer would get deeply into debt. It caused enormous resentment and it is interesting to know that when the Jewish people revolted against the Roman occupation, one of the first things they did was to burn the debt records in Jerusalem. By putting relationships first, Jesus was of course encouraging the farmers to work together to make sure that the tactics of the rich would not work.

CONCLUSION

The way we handle money and possessions says an awful lot about us. We only have to think about the amount of time we spend each day earning, spending, saving, giving and worrying about money to realise that. In our society we have to be seen to be successful (driving the 'right' car, living in the 'right' area) and this causes immense pressure. But Jesus warns us to hold on to his values, not the values of this world. He tells us to sacrifice things on earth so that we can store up eternal treasures. He warns of the real dangers of wealth, he demonstrates that forgiveness is paramount, and shows that we really can use money and possessions in the service of Christ and others.

For God's sake, for your sake and for the sake of the hungry, lost and hurting, I hope that this book will have helped you to take a look at money and possessions from Christ's perspective and then enable you to go forward with his priorities.

Debt Free Living – A book for all who face money worries – and for those who help them.

- *Overdue bills?*
- *Too many credit cards?*
- *Worrying letters from your bank manager?*
- *Rows at home over money?*

Today it is all too easy to get into debt. Banks and building societies offer generous loans. Consumer goods come with interest-free credit. We are tempted to measure our self-worth by what we own.

This book shows how you, or a friend, or a family member, can get out of debt. It helps you set up a plan to establish financial discipline. It is quite possible to live *entirely debt-free*. By using principles taken from the Bible and a wealth of real-life examples, Larry Burkett and Keith Tondeur explain:

- *Personal traits that lead to debt*
- *Biblical principles on debt and borrowing*
- *A plan for paying off debts*
- *Common errors that lead to debt*
- *Credit and creditors*
- *Bankruptcy and legal options*
- *Where to find help*

LARRY BURKETT is founder and president of Christian Financial Concepts Inc., and a popular author and broadcaster.
KEITH TONDEUR is director of Credit Action in Cambridge, author of several books on finance and the National Lottery, and also a popular speaker.

Debt-Free Living
Larry Burkett and Keith Tondeur
ISBN 1 85424 367 5

MONARCH
BOOKS

Available from your local Christian Bookshop.
In case of difficulty contact Monarch Books,
Concorde House, Grenville Place, Mill Hill, London NW7 3SA